The Executive
Survival Series

Crash

and

LEARN

Julien Godbarge

Crash and [Burn] **LEARN**

A business fable about the high cost of
burnout, blind spots, and the hope of recovery
by Julien Godbarge

The Executive Survival Series

Table of Contents

Unlock the Power Inside This Book 1

Section 1: False Beliefs in the C-Suite 3

False Beliefs #1: 5
Reaching the C-Suite Will Make Us Happy

False Belief #2: 9
The C-Suite Will Silence Our Inner Critic

False Belief #3: 15
Reaching the C-Suite Will Erase Our Past Failures and Trauma

False Belief #4: 21
Everybody Wants the C-Suite, and Only a Select Few Deserve to Be There

False Belief #5: 25
The C-Suite Will Make Us Indispensable and Give Us Ultimate Control

Summary: 31
The Five False Beliefs That Quietly Shape Executive Burnout

Section 2: Jason Marchand - CEO 35

Chapter 1 37
Flag Day

Chapter 2 51
Junior CEO

Chapter 3 63
Deal Fever

Chapter 4 77
More Shelf Space

Chapter 5 85
High Stakes, Higher Pressure

Chapter 6 93
Closing Deals, Ignoring Signals

Chapter 7 101
Everything is Fine

Chapter 8 109
Ignition Point

Chapter 9 117
Crash and Burn

Chapter 10 127
After the Freefall

Chapter 11 131
The Offer

Chapter 12 135
Boundaries

Chapter 13 139
Leadership After Ego

Section 3: Ten Blind Spots that Lead to Burnout 143

Introduction to the Blind Spots 145

Blind Spot #1: 147
The Denial Tax - Ignoring Early Warning Signals

Blind Spot #2: 155
The Confidence Pendulum – From Hubris to Imposter Syndrome

Blind Spot #3: 163
The Focus Fallacy – Activity ≠ Strategy

Blind Spot #4: 169
Performance-Based Worth - Worth Tied to Achievement & Status

Blind Spot #5: 177
The Judgment Trap - Emotional Reactivity vs. Discernment

Blind Spot #6: 183
Perfectionism's Prison - Impossible Standards

Blind Spot #7: 191
The Isolation Trap – Atlas Syndrome

Blind Spot #8: 195
Transactional Relationships - The Erosion of Authentic Connection

Blind Spot #9: 201
Boundary Collapse - Work Consuming All of Life

Blind Spot #10: 207
The Competence Illusion – Confusing Knowledge with Practice

Section 4: The Reset 211

From Awareness to Integration: How Leaders Rebuild from the Inside Out 213

Work with Julien 219

Resources & Tools 221

Acknowledgments 223

About the Author 227

Glossary 229

Crash and [Burn] **LEARN**

The Executive Survival Series

Printed in the United States of America

Cover Design: Ares Jun

Formatting: Aubree Valentine with Beyond the Bookshelf Publishing

For information about special discounts for bulk purchases, please contact Julien Godbarge at jgodbarge@gemconsultingsolutions.com

---

Business Fable Disclaimer: This book is written as a business fable, a creative nonfiction structure that combines real business principles with storytelling elements to enhance learning and retention. While the lessons and frameworks presented are based on the author's decades of business experience and genuine insights gained from successful mentors, the specific conversations, characters, situations, and scenarios described may have been dramatized, reconstructed, and in some cases fictionalized for educational and narrative purposes.

Any resemblance to actual persons, living or deceased, specific companies, or particular business situations is illustrative in nature. The characters referenced throughout this book represent the embodiment of wisdom gained over the author's career.

Results Disclaimer: The business strategies, techniques, and principles described in this book reflect the experiences and opinions of the author. The results achieved by the individuals referenced in this book are their own and should not be considered typical or guaranteed. Individual results will vary based on numerous factors, including but not limited to personal effort, market conditions, business environment, individual circumstances, and the consistent application of the principles described.

The author and publisher make no representations or warranties regarding the potential results, financial or otherwise, that may be achieved through the application of the methods described in this book. Readers should consult qualified professionals before making significant business or financial decisions based on the content.

Educational Purpose: This book is intended for educational and informational purposes only, except for the occasional entertainment value the reader may experience. The author and publisher disclaim any liability for decisions made or actions taken based on the information provided in this book.

To Sharon, my wife, whose unconditional love and support never wavered through the meteoric rise, the spectacular crash, and the rebuilding that followed.

To Harry Whaley, mentor and guide, who shaped the first chapter of my career with brilliance and wisdom that still lights my path.

To Kae Wagner, writing partner and editor extraordinaire, without whom these words would remain unwritten and these lessons unshared.

And to every executive navigating the treacherous waters of success: may the blind spots that nearly destroyed me become the signposts that guide you safely to your destination.

Crash and [Burn] LEARN

This nonfiction business book fable blends real stories, real pressure, and the raw truth of what happens when a high-achieving leader finally hits his breaking point.

What follows is part narrative, part inside look at the mental patterns that quietly steer a career toward burnout, and part exploration of the blind spots that create a devastating spiral; followed by practical steps that put the pieces back together.

You're about to step into scenes, conversations, and decisions that feel uncomfortably familiar. That's the point. It's a lived experience, distilled so you can see yourself clearly and move forward with more awareness, more clarity, and a more sustainable path to success.

Unlock the Power Inside This Book

Crush and [Burn] ***LEARN*** is designed to challenge you, confront you, and, if you let it, evolve the way you lead. This isn't a "read once and nod" kind of book. It's a tool. And tools only work when you pick them up with intention.

Section 1 exposes the false beliefs that quietly drive so many high-achieving leaders into exhaustion. Read these slowly. Notice which ones make you bristle, which ones feel eerily familiar, and which ones hit a little too close to home. Those reactions aren't random. They're data. They show you where your own patterns might be running the show.

Then you'll follow Jason Marchand in Section 2, a fictionalized CEO who I know all too well. His spiral mirrors what thousands of leaders experience behind closed doors. Don't read his story as entertainment. Read it as a mirror. Where do your instincts match his? Where do your habits differ? Where does your mind whisper, "Oh... I've done that"?

Section 3 is where the work gets real. The ten Blind Spots reveal the cognitive, emotional, and behavioral traps that keep even the smartest leaders stuck. Treat this section like your personal diagnostic. Pause after each blind spot. Ask yourself: *Where does this show up for me? How much is it costing me? What would shift if I interrupted this pattern?* At the end of the book, you'll be invited to access The Ten Blind Spots assessment.

Finally, Section 4 will pull everything together. It gives you the language, the practices, and the next steps to move forward with clarity instead of chaos. By the time you reach the Glossary and "What to Do Next," you'll know exactly the pattern that's limiting you and how to interrupt it.

Take your time. Take notes. And above all, stay honest with yourself. The leaders who get the most from this book are the ones willing to look straight at the truth, even when it stings a little. That's when the real transformation begins.

Section 1: False Beliefs in the C-Suite

False Belief #1: REACHING THE C-SUITE WILL MAKE US HAPPY

I used to believe happiness lived somewhere out ahead of me. Waiting. Hiding behind a title, a paycheck, or the next shiny milestone. It's a seductive lie, especially for people wired like us. Top performers love a finish line.

But here's the thing about happiness. It's not waiting for us at the top of the corporate ladder. And nothing about reaching the C-Suite, those corner offices on the top floor that are the goal of so many, magically flips that happiness switch inside us.

In fact, most executives only realize this after they've spent decades sprinting toward a fantasy.

Real Talk About How We Chase Happiness

The Greeks were arguing about happiness long before any of us were fighting for budget approvals or board support.

They saw two competing roads:

Epicurean living. Chase pleasure. Pour the wine. Indulge the senses. The idea is simple. Maximize delight, feel good, keep feeling good.

Ataraxia. Strip cravings down. Remove the noise. Let go of wanting. Find peace by needing less, not more.

Most of us swing between those poles without even realizing it. More pleasure on one end. Less craving on the other. Neither extreme work for long. The sweet spot is personal. Some executives find it through simplicity. Others through indulgence. Most never stop long enough to understand their own pattern.

But here's where the lie becomes dangerous. We act like happiness is waiting on the other side of achievement. Like the next promotion will finally calm the restlessness. Like success will soothe whatever hasn't felt settled inside us for years.

It won't.

Why Pleasure Doesn't Deliver the Happiness We Expect

Pleasure has a predictable pattern in the brain. Dopamine floods your system when you get something delightful. It spikes. It feels great. Then it drops. Often below baseline.

That drop is where craving comes from.

Some people tolerate those swings better than others. Some chase the next spike before the crash even hits. And some convince themselves that if they just achieve more, the drop won't hurt as much.

But it always does.

That's the cycle executives get trapped in. The hit from the promotion doesn't last. The office upgrade doesn't land the way we expected. Even the big wins feel strangely hollow. Yet we keep going back to the same strategy, assuming we just haven't "hit the right goal" yet.

The Real Question Behind Every Goal

This book isn't here to moralize pleasure. It's here to help you stop lying to yourself about why you want certain things.

Every goal hides a deeper reason. Sometimes a beautiful one. Sometimes not.

Two people can want the same thing for completely different motives.

One wants a boat because the water is their sanctuary. The other wants a boat because the executives they admire all have one at the marina.

Same purchase. Very different paths. Only one leads to actual happiness.

That's the power of the "Russian Doll" approach. Keep asking why until you hit the truth. Not the glossy reason you give in job interviews. The real one.

Why do you want the C-Suite title?

Why do you think it will make you happy?

And why is that?

Keep peeling. Eventually you'll hit the core. It might surprise you.

The Brutal Truth About Happiness

Happiness isn't waiting at a future milestone. You already carry everything you need to be happy today. That's uncomfortable for high achievers, because it removes the illusion that "the next thing" will fix whatever feels off.

And yes, there are exceptions. If you don't have food or housing security, future improvements really can shift happiness. But if you're reading a book about burnout in the C-Suite, that's not the situation you're in.

So, the challenge becomes honesty. What are you chasing because it genuinely lights you up? And what are you chasing because you've been conditioned to believe it should?

I'll be honest. I'd probably enjoy a country club membership. Tennis courts. Pool. Lunch on a sunny patio. It sounds great. But making it a mental finish line? A marker of arrival? Something that steals hours of my life fantasizing about it. No. That's where I draw the line.

Wanting isn't the problem. Believing happiness lives on the other side of achievement is.

The C-Suite won't deliver happiness you haven't built inside yourself. Jason Marchand learned that the hard way in his hell-bent fixation on acquisitions.

It may amplify what's already working. But it will definitely magnify whatever you haven't dealt with.

You deserve to know the difference before you chase the next big milestone. Because this first false belief is the one that sets up all the others.

False Belief #2:
THE C-SUITE WILL SILENCE OUR INNER CRITIC

I used to think the C-Suite would finally shut that voice up. You know the one. The quiet whisper that shows up right after a big win and tells you it wasn't enough. Or that you only succeeded because the timing was lucky. Or that someone smarter would have done it better.

Most executives carry that voice around like a second spine. We get so used to it that we mistake it for motivation. We let it push us. Prod us. Shame us into going harder. And we convince ourselves that once we get high enough in our career, the voice will fade.

It won't.

If anything, it gets louder.

Real Talk About Imposter Syndrome

If you're human, you've had moments where part of you believes you're one step away from being exposed. It doesn't matter how much evidence you've collected to the contrary. It doesn't matter how many results you've delivered.

That inner critic has one job. Doubt.

You look at your performance. You see the metrics, the outcomes, the promotions. Your rational brain says, "I earned this."

Then the voice sneaks in.

"Yes, but someone else did it faster."

"Yes, but your competitor had a disastrous year."

"Yes, but you're still not as sharp as the COO who left last quarter."

That voice is relentless. And it always finds a comparison that tilts the scale against you. If you let it speak unchecked, it will rewrite your entire identity.

How the Voice Changes the Way We Climb

There's a predictable pattern executives fall into.

We tell ourselves the next project will be the one that proves we're legitimate. The next promotion will be the one that finally makes us feel worthy. The next big initiative will erase every doubt.

We take the assignment and grind through it. We deliver, get praised, and rewarded. And then what?

The voice returns. Same tone. Same script. Same erosion.

No, that wasn't the one. But the next one will be.

This cycle repeats every three to five years. Which also happens to be the average length of time most leaders stay in a role before the next step up.

By the time we're in line for the C-Suite, we've lived through this loop so many times we've internalized a dangerous assumption.

This one will finally shut the critic down once and for all.

It won't. Because the critic isn't tied to the work. It's tied to the wound that shaped the voice to begin with.

Why Listening to the Voice Backfires

The voice feels useful. That is part of the trap.

It keeps us sharp.

It keeps us driven.

It keeps us hungry.

That's the mythology, but here's the truth that executives don't like admitting.

The inner critic doesn't fuel excellence. It fuels tension.

And that tension becomes structural. It embeds itself in your identity. It becomes the operating system that powers your ambition. You build a tower of success on top of unstable emotional footing, and because the tower keeps rising, you convince yourself the foundation is fine.

Until it isn't.

What Happens at the Top

When you finally step into the C-Suite, the voice doesn't congratulate you. It recalibrates.

"You got the title. Now you'd better prove you deserved it."

"Everyone is watching."

"One mistake and they'll know."

The intensity increases because the stakes increase.

That's why so many executives find themselves burning out not before the C-Suite, but shortly after arriving. The voice has been building pressure for decades. It finally reaches critical mass at the very moment you expected relief.

The irony isn't lost on me. I lived it.

The Only Way The Voice Ever Quiets

There's no title in the corporate world that can silence your inner critic. None.

The only thing that works is rewiring the relationship altogether.

That starts by understanding what type of critic you're dealing with. Then by interrupting the patterns it uses to hijack your thinking. And finally, by replacing its messages with something grounded in reality rather than fear.

This is not soft psychological theory. It is cognitive rewiring. When you build new neural pathways, you permanently weaken the old ones.

It is the first thing I do with every executive I coach because nothing else changes until this changes.

You cannot out-achieve or outrun the voice. Nor can you bury it under success.

You have to confront it directly.

Why This Matters Right Now

If you believe the C-Suite will finally validate you, you're wrong. You're stepping into the most demanding role of your life with a flawed expectation that will drain you instead of strengthening you.

The C-Suite magnifies what's already inside you.

If your inner critic is running the show today, it will run the boardroom tomorrow.

You deserve better than that. And the people you lead deserve a version of you who isn't battling invisible sabotage during every decision.

Addressing your internal thoughts is the work that changes

everything. I've watched leaders transform entire careers by rewiring this single pattern.

You don't need a different title. You need a different inner voice.

False Belief #3:
REACHING THE C-SUITE WILL ERASE OUR PAST FAILURES AND TRAUMA

I wish this one were true. I really do. Because if any belief has pulled high performers through years of pressure, it is the fantasy that success can redeem everything that came before it:

The embarrassing missteps.

The humiliations we never talked about.

The layoffs we executed and still think about at night.

The promotions we didn't get.

The meetings where we froze.

The childhood bruises we pretend no longer matter.

We like to pretend those things dissolve as we rise. But the truth? They follow us. Quietly. Patiently. Sometimes for decades.

And they grow if we don't deal with them.

How Trauma Sneaks into the Executive Suite

People assume trauma means catastrophic events. Something dramatic. Something in the movies.

But trauma is anything your nervous system couldn't process at the time it happened. Anything that overwhelmed you. Anything you shoved aside because you were too busy performing to feel it.

Executives are world-class avoiders. We learned early on how to power through stress. We learned how to outrun discomfort. And because that strategy got rewarded, we never questioned it.

But here's the thing about the human body. It always keeps score. Even when we refuse to.

The Stress Cycle that Almost No One Completes

Thousands of years ago, the stress cycle worked perfectly.

Threat appeared. The body spiked adrenaline and cortisol. Energy surged. Fight or flee. Threat ended.

Hormones returned to baseline. Cycle complete.

But modern stress rarely ends cleanly. You don't get chased by a tiger. You get chased by unresolved conversations, silent pressures, impossible timelines, shifting priorities, and disappointments you pretend didn't sting.

Stress rises. It peaks. And instead of resolving, it lingers.

Your body lowers the alarm a little. But not all the way.

Your baseline becomes a little higher. Then the next stressor hits. Higher again. Then another.

Higher still.

Twenty years go by, and your baseline has quietly climbed from one to a four. Or a six.

You think you are managing well because nothing has exploded. But your system is bracing constantly, and you don't even know it.

The Hidden Emotional Debt Executives Carry

Every unprocessed event adds to a tab your nervous system keeps track of in the background.

Do you recognize these?

The betrayal you skipped over. The job you lost but never grieved. The marriage strains you stuffed under your work ethic. The shame of being blindsided in a board meeting. The fear from that hostile takeover attempt. The guilt from letting people go in a recession.

You might forget the details. Your body never forgets the load.

This is emotional debt. And like financial debt, it compounds over time.

Executives often hit their highest roles with the highest accumulated balance. Which is why burnout at the top looks sudden from the outside but feels inevitable from the inside.

Why the C-Suite Makes This Worse, Not Better

Many leaders believe the title will turn their history into fuel. That prestige will reframe the failures. That compensation will make the sacrifices feel justified.

But trauma doesn't convert to triumph just because you have a corner office.

In the C-Suite, the baseline stress you've been carrying for years collides with a whole list of challenges you didn't see coming:

Higher public scrutiny.

Bigger decisions.

Unrelenting visibility.

More stakeholders.

Less margin for error.

Fewer safe spaces to breathe.

You walk in thinking you've made it. Your nervous system walks in thinking it is surrounded by threat.

That mismatch is why so many executives collapse emotionally within the first three years of reaching the job they worked their entire lives to get.

Their system wasn't broken. It was overloaded.

What This Looked Like for Me

There was a point in my career when I genuinely believed success would absolve everything. I thought the right promotion would finally make the painful chapters worth it. I thought it would lift the weight of every previous failure.

But the moment I got the title, I realized something unsettling.

Those unresolved experiences didn't disappear. They amplified. My shame got louder. My fear got sharper. My internal pressure skyrocketed. I reached the job that should have given me confidence. Instead, I felt the cracks in my foundation widening.

That was the moment I understood the truth. Success doesn't heal unprocessed pain. It exposes it.

Why This Matters for You

If you are climbing the ladder believing the C-Suite will finally untangle the knots in your past, you are not climbing toward relief. You are climbing toward acceleration.

Everything that is unresolved accelerates at the top. Everything that is unexamined intensifies.

Everything you avoid becomes impossible to outrun.

This is not a warning meant to discourage you. It is an invitation to stop carrying a load that doesn't belong on your back anymore.

There are ways to complete those unfinished stress cycles. Ways to lower your baseline. Ways to process experiences that you've been holding in your jaw and shoulders for years. Ways to lead without dragging your entire emotional history behind you like armor you never asked for.

But the first step is rejecting this false belief.

The C-Suite cannot erase your past.

Only you can.

False Belief #4:

EVERYBODY WANTS THE C-SUITE, AND ONLY A SELECT FEW DESERVE TO BE THERE

There's a quiet assumption inside most high performers. We rarely say it out loud, but we behave like it's true.

"Everyone wants the C-Suite. Only the exceptional make it."

It sounds noble. It sounds ambitious. It sounds like something that should motivate us.

But here's the truth I wish someone had told me earlier.

Wanting the C-Suite has very little to do with talent. And even less to do with what will actually make you fulfilled once you get there.

The real divide is not between exceptional and average. It's between the people who are wired for C-Suite life and the people who are capable of it but miserable once they get in the chair.

Real Talk About Capability Versus Preference

Executives tend to confuse the two.

Capability says you *can* do the job. Preference says you would actually enjoy the job.

These are not the same things. For example:

You can be exceptional at strategic thinking and still hate the time horizon of long-range planning.

You can be a gifted communicator who dreads managing external stakeholders.

You can be brilliant at your craft and still feel empty once the role distances you from it.

The higher you climb, the more the job becomes about fit, not brilliance.

And most leaders never pause long enough to ask the simple question that would save them years of stress.

Do I actually want the life that comes with this title?

The Planning Horizon That Surprises Most Leaders

Let's start with the part no one explains well.

The C-Suite doesn't live in the present. It barely lives in the current quarter. Almost everything you work on unfolds three years out. Sometimes five. Sometimes longer.

By the time a CEO is celebrating quarterly earnings, they are mentally three fiscal years ahead. They're not in the moment you see. They're in the one that hasn't arrived yet.

If you get your energy from solving today's fires, leading from the trenches, or being in the mix of the actual work, the C-Suite can feel like exile. You're planning for a future you may never see executed. And you spend very little time inside the action that brought you joy in the first place.

The irony is that many leaders only realize this after they get the title. And by then it's too complicated to admit the truth.

"I don't enjoy this the way I thought I would."

The Stakeholder Shift No One Warns You About

Before you enter the C-Suite, most of your focus is internal on your team, projects, and failures.

Once you step into the executive level, your world flips.

Your audience becomes the people outside your walls.

Investors who expect both vision and predictability.

Board members with opinions shaped by past scars you never saw.

Banking partners watching every number.

Regulators who can change your path overnight.

Journalists who can magnify misinterpretations in a single headline.

You are suddenly expected to communicate flawlessly, negotiate constantly, and stay composed while a dozen external pressures collide.

You might be capable of this. But do you enjoy it? Does it energize you or drain you?

That question matters more than anyone wants to admit.

The Loss Nobody Talks About

Most executives rose through a craft.

Engineering, finance, marketing, sales, operations, for example. Your craft is what made you valuable. It is where you earned confidence. It is what made you feel like yourself.

The C-Suite takes you further from it with every step.

You still use your experience. You still bring perspective. But you no longer do the work you loved. You oversee it. From a distance. A different altitude.

For some people, that's liberation. For others, it feels like losing a limb.

I didn't expect the ache that came with that distance. Many don't. You might not either. That's why these questions matter before you chase the title, not after.

The Real Myth Under the Myth

The dangerous belief isn't that only a few people make it to the top. The dangerous belief is that everyone *should* want to.

The C-Suite is not a universal destination. It is a niche environment. It rewards certain temperaments. It punishes others. It offers meaning to some leaders and steals meaning from others.

Just because you can thrive there does not mean the role aligns with what keeps your inner life healthy. And just because the world celebrates the title doesn't mean the life behind that title matches the life you actually want.

You owe yourself the honesty to separate your competence from your desire.

A New Question to Ask Yourself

Instead of asking, "Am I exceptional enough for the C-Suite?"

Try this instead. "Is the C-Suite aligned with the version of myself I want to live with?"

Ambition without self-awareness is a straight shot to burnout. Ambition with clarity is rocket fuel.

This belief is one of the easiest to dismantle and one of the most liberating to challenge. Once you do, the path forward becomes yours again, not the path you inherited from expectations you never consented to.

False Belief #5:

THE C-SUITE WILL MAKE US INDISPENSABLE AND GIVE US ULTIMATE CONTROL

There is a belief many high performers carry quietly, almost like a secret promise they made to themselves early in their careers. It goes something like this.

"If I can make it far enough. If I can earn the title and take the seat at the table where the biggest decisions are made, then I will finally have control. I will finally be the one calling the shots instead of reacting to them."

It is one of the most compelling myths in corporate life because it feels so logical.

Every promotion seems to give us a little more authority. Every new responsibility seems to widen the arena where our voice matters. It is easy to assume that this pattern continues in a straight line, and that the highest roles will naturally offer the highest level of autonomy.

But the truth at the top is very different from the fantasy that fuels the climb.

The Illusion of Control That Follows Us Up the Ladder

As leaders rise through the ranks, they naturally begin to believe their influence is synonymous with control. It is not an ego problem. It is simply the lived experience of achievement.

You make decisions and people execute them.

You shape a strategy and teams move in that direction.

You steer a department and watch it transform under your leadership.

Over time, it becomes easy to think that the ability to shape outcomes defines your leadership. And when you have lived through enough cycles of success, you begin to assume that more authority means more control.

What I learned the hard way is that influence and control begin to diverge the moment you reach the executive level. They do not rise in tandem. They start moving in opposite directions.

Where Grandiosity Sneaks In

Bestselling author Robert Greene, the authority on power and human nature, writes about grandiosity, the human tendency to inflate our sense of power as our achievements accumulate.

Executives are particularly vulnerable to this because our careers are built on a long trail of wins. Every success reinforces the idea that we are uniquely capable. Every promotion becomes evidence that we see farther, think faster, and understand the business in ways others cannot.

It feels good. It feels earned. And because it feels earned, it often goes unchallenged.

But there is a danger when confidence crosses into inflated perception. Not because confidence is bad, but because it creates a blind spot around the simple truth that no executive controls the environment they lead.

The company, the market, and the broader world are too complex for any one individual to command. Even the most capable leaders are operating inside forces far larger than themselves.

The Reality of Constraints at the Top

From the outside, the C-Suite looks like pure freedom. Once you are in the chair, people assume you can move the company in any direction you want.

Inside the role, the experience is very different.

You are accountable to a board that can remove you if your strategy does not align with their expectations. You must balance investor pressures, customer needs, competitive threats, regulatory frameworks, and shifting economic conditions that no one can predict with precision. You must navigate reputational risks that can surface in a single headline and undo years of progress.

The job expands your responsibility dramatically, yet your actual levers of control become more limited, more constrained, and more dependent on forces outside your influence.

It is an odd and uncomfortable paradox.

You feel the weight of accountability more intensely than at any previous point in your career, yet you have fewer direct mechanisms to shape outcomes. Many leaders are not prepared for that imbalance when they enter the role.

The Myth of Being Indispensable

Another quiet belief many executives carry is the idea that reaching the top will finally make them irreplaceable. It is comforting to imagine that decades of sacrifice will culminate in a position where the company cannot function without you.

But here is the part that rarely gets said out loud.

The higher the position, the easier it is to replace the person in it.

Companies replace CEOs and CFOs with surprising regularity, not because they are incompetent, but because circumstances change. A new board comes in. A merger shifts strategic priorities. The market demands a different leadership profile. Sometimes it is simply timing.

Good executives get replaced. Exceptional executives get replaced. The system is designed to ensure continuity regardless of who occupies the chair.

When you understand this, the pursuit of indispensability becomes less about security and more about ego. And ego is a fragile foundation for long-term leadership.

Why Control Shrinks as Scope Expands

When you lead a team, you can walk into a room and directly influence a problem. You see the levers. You pull them. You get immediate feedback.

At the executive level, there is distance between you and the work. You lead through layers, through culture, through systems that have inertia of their own. Your decisions take months or years to reveal their impact. Success depends on alignment across hundreds or thousands of people you do not observe on a daily basis.

Your job becomes less about direct action and more about orchestrating an ecosystem that will execute without your constant presence. It is an entirely different skill. And it is far less controllable.

Once this reality lands, some executives feel a sense of disorientation. Others feel exposed. A few feel liberated. But almost everyone realizes they were operating under an assumption that does not match the lived experience of the job.

The Cost of Believing the Myth

When a leader enters the C-Suite believing it will grant control, they often react poorly when the opposite proves true.

They double down on authority, make unilateral decisions, and push harder instead of listening more carefully. They begin resisting outside feedback, not because they are arrogant, but because their internal model of leadership has just collided with reality.

This is when burnout accelerates. Pressure rises. Relationships fray. The job begins to feel hostile instead of empowering.

I have watched brilliant leaders crack under the weight of this misconception.

Where Real Power Lives

Over time, most successful executives come to understand that genuine power does not come from control. It comes from clarity. It comes from steady influence. It comes from being able to navigate complexity rather than dominate it.

Real power is the ability to stay grounded while the world around you shifts.

It is the ability to build systems that remain stable even when external forces are volatile.

It is the ability to cultivate teams that think well, challenge you honestly, and operate with discipline independent of your presence.

It is the ability to communicate with integrity even when your decisions are unpopular.

Control is brittle. Influence is durable.

One snaps under pressure. The other adapts.

Why This Shift Matters

If you enter the C-Suite believing the title will give you unshakeable control, the job will feel like a betrayal.

If you enter understanding that leadership at the highest level is an exercise in influence, adaptability, and humility, you will navigate the role with far more stability and far less emotional friction.

The C-Suite cannot give you the security or permanence you may secretly hope it will.

What it can give you, if you approach it with the right expectations, is a vantage point where you can make meaningful impact without letting the mythology of control distort your leadership.

That shift in understanding is what allows a leader not only to survive the C-Suite, but to thrive within it.

Summary:
THE FIVE FALSE BELIEFS THAT QUIETLY SHAPE EXECUTIVE BURNOUT

If there is one thread running through all five false beliefs, it is this.

Most of us spend our entire careers chasing feelings we assume will arrive at the top. We believe happiness will finally land once the title is ours.

We believe the voice inside our head will soften and that our past will lose its grip. We believe the role will fit us simply because we are capable of performing it.

And we believe control will expand in direct proportion to our success.

These beliefs are comforting. They help us endure long seasons of pressure. They make the sacrifices feel meaningful. But they all share the same flaw.

They project internal needs onto external achievements.

Happiness is not delivered by accomplishment.

Self-worth is not earned through performance.

Trauma does not dissolve in corner offices.

Preference is not the same as capability.

And control does not expand just because responsibility does.

Executives rarely challenge these assumptions while they are climbing, because the climb itself rewards momentum over introspection. The system incentivizes movement. Promotions. Bigger goals. Larger teams. More scope. Very few people pause long enough to notice what is happening inside them while all of this unfolds.

By the time leaders reach the C-Suite, these unexamined beliefs have been running quietly in the background for years. When reality does not match fantasy, it creates a shock that many interpret as personal failure, when it is actually the collapse of a flawed internal model.

The emotional turbulence that shows up at the top is not a sign of weakness. It is the natural outcome of building a career on assumptions that were never true to begin with.

This is the moment where a different kind of work begins. One of understanding what actually drives your happiness. Of rewriting the inner voice that has been pushing you for decades and the acknowledging and processing the experiences your body has held long after your mind moved on.

The inner work deepens with deciding whether the environment you are striving for aligns with who you are, not who you think you should be.

It is when you shift from the illusion of control to the practice of grounded influence.

When you dismantle these beliefs, something powerful happens. The C-Suite stops being a proving ground or a finish line. It becomes a place where you can lead without dragging unresolved weight behind you. You begin to reclaim the parts of yourself that success never actually replaced. And you start building a career defined not by pressure, but by clarity.

This is where real leadership begins. Not because of the title or the corner office.

Leadership lies in the willingness to examine the hidden beliefs that shaped your climb and choose something truer, and far healthier, for the road ahead.

What Happens When These False Beliefs Collide With Reality

By now, you've seen how the five false beliefs shape the inner world of high performers. You may have recognized pieces of your own story in them. Most executives do. These beliefs are subtle. They operate quietly. And they have a way of becoming the architecture beneath an entire career without us realizing.

Principles and insights only take us so far. Sometimes we need a wake-up call to break these beliefs to see and understand their full impact.

Jason Marchand, aka me, Julien Godbarge, was one of those lives.

On paper, he was exactly what the system rewards. Exceptional performer. Relentless worker. Strategic thinker. Someone who always delivered, always adapted, always kept moving. He believed in all five false promises, not because he was naive, but because the world around him reinforced them at every turn.

He believed the C-Suite would make him happy and the title would silence the voice that kept telling him he hadn't done enough.

He believed success would finally justify the scars of earlier failures. He just knew he was destined for the top because he could operate at that level. And he believed that once he got there, he would finally have control.

He was wrong. And the cost of that misunderstanding broke him.

Jason's story is not a cautionary tale meant to shame ambition. It is a story about what happens when a brilliant, capable, well-meaning leader builds an entire life on false beliefs that collapse when sustained pressure quietly crosses an invisible threshold.

It is a story about burnout that didn't appear out of nowhere but grew silently under the surface long before the world saw the crash.

His story matters because it is the lived version of everything we have just explored. It is the proof.

The human evidence. The wake-up call wrapped inside a single career.

But it is also something else.

Jason's story is proof that recovery is possible and that self-awareness is teachable. It shows that the C-Suite office is not enemy territory to be abandoned, but that it can be sacred ground on which ego and blind spots are burned at the altar.

It shows that clarity can be rebuilt. That leadership is not defined by whether you fall, but whether you understand why you fell and what you choose to do next.

In the next part of this book, Section Two, we shift from insight to narrative, where we see how the inner workings of the mind lead to the unfolding of a life.

We're going from the theory of burnout to the journey of someone who lived it, survived it, and learned from it.

Let's step into Jason Marchand's world and walk with him through the rise, the crash, and the difficult, humbling, necessary rebuilding that followed.

This is where the real story begins.

Section 2:
Jason Marchand - CEO

Chapter One

FLAG DAY

Jason Marchand stood at his desk, finger hovering over the refresh button. Nothing. He clicked again. Still nothing.

The open-space office hummed with the usual mid-morning energy. Phones ringing. Keyboards clacking. Someone laughing too loud near the break room. Jason heard none of it. His entire world had narrowed to a single question: had his boss, Bob Harrigan, sent the email yet?

He'd been at Horizon Brands for over a decade. Started as Export Manager right out of grad school, back when the company was a fraction of its current size. Now they did business in forty countries, employed three hundred people, and had a private equity firm breathing down Bob's neck about growth targets.

Jason had delivered. Every single time.

He managed the launch of two new product lines. Kept sales moving during the financial crisis when every other brand manager was drowning. Took over two underperforming brands and turned them around in eighteen months.

And now, finally, his reward.

The Toronto subsidiary. A real leadership role. Managing Director of the Canadian operation.

He refreshed again.

There it was.

Subject: Org Change

His heart kicked. He would've jumped out of his chair if he hadn't already been at his stand-up desk. Instead, he reached into his drawer and pulled out the neatly folded Canadian flag he'd stashed there two days ago.

He'd planned this moment down to the last detail.

The flag clips hooked perfectly onto the drop ceiling grid above his cubicle partition. He unfurled it with a snap, red and white filling the air above his workspace. Then he grabbed the scarf from his bag, red and white wool with maple leaves scattered across the pattern and wrapped it around his neck.

Perfect.

The whispers started immediately. Heads popped up over cubicle walls like prairie dogs. Someone laughed. Someone else started clapping.

Jason grinned.

Within minutes, a small crowd had gathered. High-fives, several hugs. A few people pulled out their phones for pictures. Jason stood in the center of it all, flag overhead, scarf around his neck, soaking in every second.

"Congrats, man. You earned this," Mike from logistics said.

"About time they recognized what you've been doing," Sarah from marketing added.

Jason's phone buzzed.

A text from his boss:

Well deserved. Let's talk later this week about moving forward on the transition timeline.

He showed the text to a few people nearby. More congratulations. More pats on the back.

This was it. This was what all the late nights and weekend strategy sessions and missed soccer games had been building toward. A real title. Real authority. A business unit that mattered.

He spent the rest of the day riding the high. Emails to the Toronto team introducing himself. Calls with the outgoing Managing Director to map the transition. A celebratory lunch with his closest colleagues, where they reminisced about the early days and toasted to what came next.

By the time Jason packed up his bag and headed to the parking lot, the adrenaline had started to fade. The thirty-minute drive to his house gave him too much time to think.

His house was on a tree-lined street in the nicer part of Pittsburgh. Four thousand square feet of renovated charm. Original hardwood floors. Italian marble in the kitchen. A backyard big enough to host the summer barbecues that made all the neighbors jealous.

He'd worked his ass off for this house. And now he hated coming home to it.

Jason pulled into the driveway, killed the engine, and sat for a moment. Through the front window he could see the chandelier in the dining room, the one his wife had insisted on. It cost more than his first car.

He grabbed his bag and walked inside.

"Hey," he called out.

No answer.

The kids were at after-school activities. His wife was probably upstairs. She spent a lot of time upstairs lately.

Jason dropped his bag by the door and walked into the kitchen. He opened the fridge, stared at its contents without seeing anything, and closed it again.

He should feel good right now. He should feel like celebrating.

Instead, he felt the familiar knot in his stomach, the one that appeared every time he walked through this door.

Footsteps on the stairs. His wife appeared in the doorway, arms crossed.

"How was your day?" she asked. Her tone was flat.

"Good. I got the promotion. Toronto."

"Congratulations."

She didn't sound like she meant it.

"It's a big deal," Jason said. "Managing Director. Real P&L responsibility."

"I know. You've been talking about it for months."

The silence stretched between them.

"We need to talk," Jason said.

"About what?"

He took a breath. "About us. About what's not working."

Her expression didn't change. "What's not working is that you're never here."

"I'm here right now."

"Physically. Sure."

Jason felt his jaw tighten. They'd had this fight before. A hundred variations of the same fight. He worked too much. She needed more. The kids needed more. Nothing he did was ever enough.

Except it was enough. It had to be. He'd built a career. Provided for his family. Had given them this house, these opportunities, this life.

"I don't want to do this anymore," Jason said.

She blinked. "Do what?"

"This. Us. I think we should separate."

The words hung in the air between them. Jason waited for the explosion. The tears. The accusations.

Instead, his wife nodded slowly. "Okay."

"Okay?"

"I'm not happy either, Jason. I haven't been for a long time."

Relief flooded through him. Not happiness. Not satisfaction. Just relief that the worst part was over.

They talked for another hour. Logistics mostly. The kids. Custody. The house. Lawyers. It was surprisingly civil, like they were negotiating a business deal instead of ending fifteen years of marriage.

By the time Jason went to bed that night, the adrenaline had fully drained. He lay in the dark, staring at the ceiling, and tried to figure out why the best day of his career felt so heavy.

The next few months moved fast. Lawyers drew up divorce papers. Jason and his wife told the kids who took it better than expected. Maybe they'd seen it coming. Maybe they were just relieved that the tension would finally end.

They put the house on the market. The Pittsburgh housing market was hot and it sold in three weeks.

Jason moved into a rental townhouse and hired a designer to "make it homey." Four bedrooms, two bathrooms, walking distance to the kids' schools. Nothing fancy, but functional. Clean. A place where he and the boys could figure out their new normal.

The custody arrangement fell into place. Week on, week off. It meant Jason could spend half his time in Toronto without disrupting the kids' routines.

He threw himself into the new role with the same intensity he'd brought to every other challenge in his career. The Toronto team was solid. Good people who knew their business. Jason's job was to give them structure, set clear goals, and get out of their way.

It worked.

Sales grew. Margins improved. Bob sent emails with words like "exceeding expectations" and "great start."

Jason started running again. Not the occasional jog to clear his head, but real training. He signed up for a marathon and built a strict schedule around it. Early morning runs before catching his flight to Toronto. Evening runs when he returned home for the weekend.

The routine kept him sane. It gave him guardrails.

He also discovered the benefits of being newly single in a mid-sized city with a thriving downtown scene. Friday nights became sacred. The weeks he didn't have the kids, he'd meet friends at Shane's 360, the Irish pub that had just opened a rooftop bar, overlooking the Allegheny River.

It was the rooftop in town with the best view, and it became their spot.

One Friday evening, about two years into the Toronto role, Jason sat on that rooftop watching the sun dip below the buildings. His best friend Sebastian sat across from him, nursing an IPA.

They'd worked together at Horizon Brands for years. Sebastian was one of the few people who understood the pressure, the politics, the constant balancing act of managing up and down simultaneously.

"Dude, did you see the numbers out of Europe?" Jason asked.

Sebastian shook his head. "Edwin's struggling."

"Struggling is generous. The guy's drowning."

Horizon Brands had acquired a UK-based distributor a few years back. It made sense on paper. European expansion. New markets. The playbook that worked everywhere else.

Except it wasn't working.

Edwin, the Managing Director, couldn't get traction. Sales were flat. Margins were terrible. And worst of all, he kept blaming headquarters for not supporting him enough.

"I was over there last month," Sebastian said. "Tried to help. They didn't want to hear it."

"Same. I spent three days in London and all I heard was complaining. Zero accountability."

"Right? Like, we're all trying to help and they act like we're the enemy."

Jason took a long sip of his beer. An idea was forming. A good one.

"You know what the difference is between Canada and Europe?" Jason said.

"What?" Sebastian said between sips of beer.

"Jodie used to visit headquarters twice a year. That was it. She ran Canada like her own kingdom, and it worked because she knew what she was doing."

"Okay."

"I'm here half the time. I'm at headquarters, in the brand meetings, in the strategy sessions. I'm the bridge between Toronto and Pittsburgh. That's why it works."

Sebastian's eyes lit up. "You're thinking what I'm thinking?"

"VP of International. I run both Canada and Europe. I can keep Canada humming and fix Europe at the same time."

"Dude. That's brilliant."

"Right? Bob trusts me. The board trusts me. I've proven I can turn things around."

"You need to pitch this."

Jason grinned. "Absolutely, can't wait to build the pitch deck!"

Two weeks later, Jason stood in Bob's corner office. Floor-to-ceiling windows overlooked the city. Bob sat behind his massive desk, reading through Jason's presentation on his iPad.

Jason had learned Bob's style over the years. He knew what mattered. Clarity. Logic. Results.

The pitch was tight. Ten slides. Clear problem statement. Concrete solution. Realistic timeline.

Bob looked up. "This makes sense."

Jason felt his pulse quicken. "I think it could really move the needle."

"Edwin's a good guy, but he's in over his head."

"I can help him. Or replace him if we need to. Either way, we'd have consistent leadership across both subsidiaries."

Bob nodded slowly. He set the iPad down and leaned back in his chair.

"I like it, Jason. I really do."

"Great. When can we make this happen?"

"That's the thing. I'm working on some big projects with the board right now. Timing isn't great for this kind of organizational change."

Jason's stomach dropped. "What kind of timeline are we talking about?"

"Let's revisit early next year."

"Next year? That's twelve months away."

"I know. But we need to pick our battles. This is a good idea. Just not right now."

Jason forced a smile. "Okay. I understand."

He did understand, but it didn't sit well. He understood that Bob was managing a hundred competing priorities and Jason's ambition wasn't at the top of the list. He understood that "next year" might as well be never in the world of corporate timelines.

He walked out of Bob's office, thanked him for his time, and made it to his car before letting himself feel the full weight of the rejection.

Not a rejection. A delay.

It felt the same.

Jason sat in the parking lot, hands on the steering wheel, staring at nothing.

He'd been at Horizon Brands for over a decade. He'd proven himself in every role. Delivered results. Exceeded expectations. And now he was supposed to sit around for a year waiting for Bob's schedule to clear?

No.

He wasn't built for waiting.

Jason pulled out of the parking lot and drove straight home to his small office in the basement. He needed a whiteboard. Space to think.

Horizon Brands had trained all their employees in Creative Problem Solving during their first six months. Jason had always loved the framework. It forced clarity. It turned messy problems into actionable steps.

He grabbed a marker and started writing.

Fuzzy: Working for one company limits growth opportunities.

Root cause: My career trajectory is subject to one CEO's timeline and priorities.

How might we: Create a career path that doesn't depend on one organization's constraints?

Jason stepped back and looked at the board.

The answer was obvious.

He couldn't scale himself within Horizon Brands. But he could scale his expertise across multiple companies.

Consulting.

He could package everything he'd learned, everything that made private equity companies fast and effective, and sell it to mid-sized regional businesses. Companies that needed help but couldn't afford a full-time executive with his background.

Jason started writing again. Faster now.

Services he could offer. Target clients. Pricing models. The elevator pitch.

By the time he left his basement office that night, he had a name: **Apex Advisory Group**.

And he had a plan.

Telling his boss was harder than telling his wife he wanted a divorce. Their relationship had blossomed early on when Jason arrived at Horizon Brands. Bob was a mentor to him.

Jason had worked for Bob for over a decade. Learned from him. Respected him deeply. The idea of walking away felt like a betrayal.

But staying felt worse.

Jason scheduled a meeting. Walked into Bob's office. Sat down.

"I'm resigning," Jason said.

Bob's expression didn't change. "You have another offer?"

"Not exactly. I'm starting a consulting firm."

"Consulting."

"Yeah. I want to take everything I've learned here and help other companies grow faster."

Bob leaned back in his chair; hands folded across his stomach. "Sounds like you've thought this through."

"I have."

"I won't try to change your mind, then."

"I appreciate that."

"You've been a great asset to this company, Jason. I mean that."

"Thank you. I learned everything from you. You've been my mentor and I have you to thank for so much."

Bob smiled. "Not everything. You brought your own fire to this place."

They shook hands. Jason walked out of the office feeling lighter than he had in months.

Building Apex Advisory was harder than Jason expected. Consulting was harder than it looked.

Networking events. Coffee meetings. Referrals that led nowhere. The first year was slow. A few small projects. Enough to keep the lights on but not enough to feel like he'd made the right call.

Then year two hit differently.

Case studies started stacking up. Referrals came faster. Jason's phone rang more often.

One of those calls came from a boutique private equity firm in Philadelphia. AFPE. Two partners, Don Henderson and Chester Brooks, who'd worked together for years.

They'd hired Jason for a few small projects in the past. Market analysis. Operational assessments. The kind of work that let them test him without committing too much.

Jason knew he was being evaluated. He didn't mind. He liked proving himself.

One afternoon, his phone buzzed with a text from Chester:

Lunch tomorrow? Don and I want to talk.

Jason replied immediately:

I'm free. What time?

The restaurant was upscale. White tablecloths. Wine list thicker than most books. Don and Chester were already seated when Jason arrived.

"Thanks for flying in," Chester said.

"Of course. Always good to see you guys."

They made small talk while the server brought water and took orders for drinks. Jason could feel the weight of something unspoken hanging in the air.

Finally, Don leaned forward. "We have a proposition for you."

"I'm listening."

"We just signed a Letter of Intent to acquire a platform company. Small operation, but solid fundamentals. Good management team, decent EBITDA, basically the business earns reliably before the accounting noise kicks in and there is room to grow with acquisitions."

Jason nodded. "Sounds promising."

"We need a CEO," Chester said. "Someone who can take it to the next level. Build the infrastructure for a roll-up."

Jason's pulse quickened. "You're offering me the role?"

"We're asking if you'd be interested."

"Where's the company located?"

"Butler, Pennsylvania."

Jason nearly laughed. "Butler? That's not far from Pittsburgh. My fiancée lives close to there."

Don and Chester exchanged a look.

"Yes, I've moved on."

"Clearly. Sounds like you won't have to relocate," Chester said. "We thought that might be an issue with your boys."

"Not even close. When can we talk details?"

They spent the next two hours mapping it out. Compensation. Equity. The vision for growth. The timeline to close.

By the time Jason walked out of that restaurant, he'd agreed to become CEO.

Not just any CEO.

The CEO of a company that would be his own platform for acquisitions. He'd have Private Equity backing, a clear growth strategy, and a five-year horizon to build something he could sell for life-changing money.

He called his fiancée from the airport.

"Hey, remember how you were going to move to Pittsburgh after your son graduates?"

"Yeah?"

"Change of plans. I'm going to be working in Butler."

She laughed. "What are you talking about?"

"I just accepted a CEO role. Company's based in Butler. We close in ninety days."

"Jason. Are you serious?"

"Dead serious."

"Oh my God." She laughed.

"I know."

He loved the lightness in her voice.

"This is happening," she said.

"This is happening, babe. It might take a few months before it's public, but this is happening."

Jason hung up and watched jets landing in the Philadelphia airport, letting it sink in.

A decade at Horizon Brands. Two years building his consulting business. And now this.

He'd arrived.

Chapter Two

JUNIOR CEO

Jason Marchand sat in his home office long after midnight, the blue glow of his laptop bouncing off half-empty coffee mugs and a clutter of legal pads. The subject line on the screen read: **CEO Employment Agreement – Final Draft.**

He'd read it three times already. Base salary, performance bonus, five-year equity vesting. The word *CEO* still looked foreign beside his name.

He scrolled to the bottom where the signature block waited. The cursor blinked like it was daring him.

He could almost hear his old boss Bob's voice: *Big titles come with big targets, Jason.*

Jason smiled. "Yeah," he murmured. "And big payouts."

He leaned back, rubbing the tension in his neck. Beyond the window, the neighbor's motion light flicked on, maybe a raccoon, maybe the universe reminding him he wasn't the only one awake. The air smelled faintly of rain and printer toner.

He pictured the email hitting Don and Chester's inboxes in the morning. *Signed. Let's go.* It was the beginning of everything he'd worked toward.

For years he'd built other people's empires. Now he'd build his own.

He clicked *Sign* before doubt could get a word in.

A soft *ding* confirmed it. Done.

Jason closed the laptop and exhaled into the dark. Tomorrow he'd start building the plan that would turn this deal into the payday of his life.

Morning came fast.

"Hey, Jason." Chester's voice over speakerphone was bright, caffeinated. "Ready to get moving?"

"Born ready." He grinned, even though no one could see it.

"Good. Don and I want you at our office on Thursday. We'll finalize the bank packet and tighten the model."

Jason scribbled the time in his notebook. "Thursday works. I'll bring my laptop and appetite."

"For deals or food?"

"Both."

Chester laughed. "Attaboy."

The line clicked off. Jason sat back, heart hammering with a mix of nerves and adrenaline. Ninety days until closing on the platform company. Ninety days to prove they'd picked the right guy.

Thursday afternoon, the conference room at AFPE smelled like fresh coffee and ambition. Chester and Don sat surrounded by spreadsheets, cash-flow forecasts, and a stack of legal pads covered in handwriting.

Jason walked in carrying his own binder. "Gentlemen. Let's make some magic."

Don raised an eyebrow. "You already sound like a CEO."

"Fake it till the wire clears," Jason said.

They laughed, tension breaking.

For hours they dissected numbers, inventory turns, margin expansions, EBITDA projections. Jason's Growth Acceleration Model was scrawled across a whiteboard by evening: three columns, five bullet points, arrows everywhere.

People. Clarity. Focus.

He explained how setting clear objectives and measuring results, the 'OKR system,' would keep everyone aligned. How a clear scoreboard could transform a culture. How they'd build scalability in twelve months; CRM, rebrand, automation, acquisitions.

Chester sat back. "You've got this mapped out like a general before battle."

"That's the idea," Jason said. "Everyone knows the plan; everyone knows their role. And the three of us know the strategy: acquire and then sell."

Don capped his pen. "All right, General. Let's make this happen."

When closing day arrived in January, Jason expected champagne and fountain pens. He thought he'd be in the room with Don and Chester, high-fiving and celebrating when they signed the acquisition papers that would finally make him CEO.

Instead, he was in his Pittsburgh home office, waiting to be notified.

"Remote closing," Chester said cheerfully on the phone. "Welcome to the future."

Jason looked around his apartment. The silence didn't exactly scream *future*. "So that's it?"

"That's it. You're officially CEO of Crestline Distribution."

Jason hung up and stared at the wall for a second, waiting for the rush to hit. It didn't.

Maybe it would when he met the team.

The next morning, he parked in front of a tan-brick building off Route 8. The small sign out front read **Crestline Distribution, Inc.**

His building now.

Inside, the air smelled faintly of metal and cardboard. Forklifts beeped somewhere behind the double doors. The receptionist, Linda, according to the placard, smiled nervously.

"You must be Jason."

"That's me."

"Welcome. Everyone's waiting in the warehouse."

Great. No easing in.

Twenty-three employees stood in a loose semicircle when he walked through the doors. There were office staff in sweaters, warehouse crew in reflective vests. Two older men flanked Jason: Frank and Dennis, the founders. Both looked equal parts proud and exhausted.

Frank cleared his throat. "Folks, Dennis and I are retiring. The company's been acquired by a private equity firm. This is Jason Marchand, your new CEO."

The words echoed through the open space. Someone dropped a wrench.

Jason stepped forward. "I know this is a lot to absorb. Change always is. But let me start with this, no one's losing their job. We're here to grow what you've built, not tear it down."

A few people exchanged glances. One woman, mid-forties, arms folded, spoke first. "So what changes are we talking about?"

"Good question," Jason said. "Over the next few months, I'll be learning how everything works. You all know what's great, what's painful, what needs fixing. Once we understand that together, we'll build the plan. My goal is simple: better systems, better tools, better results. Growth that creates opportunity for everyone here."

A guy in a warehouse shirt called out, "You gonna be around, or one of those CEOs who just flies in for photo ops?"

Jason smiled. "You'll get sick of seeing me."

A few chuckles rippled through the group. The tension eased an inch.

"Okay," he said. "Let's get back to making money."

That night, Jason collapsed on his couch, tie askew, phone buzzing nonstop, welcome emails from Don and Chester, vendor introductions, banker logistics. He should've been overwhelmed.

Instead, he felt alive. He texted his fiancée.

First day went well. We'll celebrate this weekend.

She texted emojis back: *thumbs up and a red heart*

He opened a notebook and wrote three words in bold letters across the top:

People. Clarity. Focus.

The next ninety days blurred into motion.

He started each morning with one-on-ones. Listened more than he talked. Wrote down everything; who hated the inventory system, who'd been running payroll manually, who secretly kept the place afloat.

Afternoons, he was on the warehouse floor, with dusty boots and sleeves rolled. He learned the routes of every driver, the quirks of every forklift, the smell of every aisle.

He hired a marketing coordinator named Jess who thought in color palettes and hashtags. She refreshed the logo, built a new website, and launched a monthly newsletter that made the team feel seen.

He replaced the ancient accounting software with something cloud-based and convinced Chester to approve Salesforce.

"Sixty grand a year," Chester said. "Worth it?"

"Completely. Data is oxygen."

By the end of the first quarter, sales were up eight percent. Anonymous employee surveys, his idea, showed morale higher than it had been in years.

Jason pinned the results to the breakroom corkboard. "This is what progress looks like," he told them. "And we're just getting started."

The beach smelled like salt and freedom. Jason and his fiancée lay side by side on lounge chairs, drinks sweating in the Caribbean sun.

"I'm glad we're here," she said. "I was afraid your new job would cancel our vacation."

Jason smiled. "Not a chance, babe. I have a good team and they are knocking it out of the park."

"You're different," she said.

"Different how?"

"Lighter. Happier. Like you finally found your lane."

He grinned behind his sunglasses. "Maybe I did."

His phone buzzed.

"Don't tell me you're checking email."

"Maybe," he said. He didn't touch his phone. But he thought about it.

Back home, the world tilted.

COVID. He'd been CEO for a year, had identified acquisition targets and now death had a grip across the entire nation.

The Texas acquisition trip on his calendar vanished overnight. Airports shut down. Supply chains buckled.

Jason sat in the Crestline conference room staring at the empty chairs of a leadership team now on Zoom.

"All right," he said, voice steady. "Here's the deal. We've got laptops, we've got the CRM, and we've got brains. We adapt, or we die. Agreed?"

Heads nodded from pixelated squares.

They went to work. Marketing tested new promotions weekly. The warehouse ran skeleton shifts with taped-off lanes and gallons of sanitizer.

Sales dipped, then stabilized, then climbed again.

When the year closed, Crestline posted record profits.

Jason looked at the numbers and felt something close to disbelief. Against every headline screaming collapse, they'd grown.

He poured a bourbon that night and stood at his kitchen window, watching rain trace lines down the glass. For the first time in a long time, he felt invincible.

He'd stared down the biggest challenge any CEO had ever faced and they'd won. Even when larger companies had faltered with the pandemic, he and his team had fought back and found higher ground.

They had beaten COVID and he could tuck the Project Pandemic file in a Banker's Box and hopefully never pull it out again.

Project names were a habit borrowed from earlier mentors. This time he gave himself permission to have fun with it. 2023 was the target year to reap the harvest from the industry roll-up plan.

Twenty-three meant one thing if you grew up where he grew up and watched the great basketball player Michael Jordan with your father on a small TV that made everything look bigger anyway.

MJ-1, he typed in the corner of the slide. It looked stupid and perfect. He let it stand.

He didn't put it on the first page of the presentation. He didn't say it out loud on the bank call. He wrote it small in his notebook and underlined it once.

On a Friday at 6:15 in the evening, with the office lights low and the empty warehouse quiet in the back like a sleeping animal, Jason watched the cursor blink on his computer. His platform, Crestline Distribution, the one Don and Chester had handed off to him, was going to make headlines in 2023.

He did the math again because doing the math again had become a way to pray.

As the world and their company pulled out of COVID's first phase of unbridled fear and angst, the office team began to trickle back in one day a week. They still maintained distance, but the success of the year had bonded them in ways that surprised Jason.

"Keep the momentum going," he'd repeat in every meeting and then again at night when he looked in the mirror.

As captain of the ship, he thought it was his duty to be on the job in the office every day. Many days he was the only one, but that didn't deter him. Someday he'd have bragging rights for weathering the storm at the helm.

One day, the phone buzzed across his desk.

Chester said on the other end, "You remember the owner in Texas? Steve? He's ready to talk again."

Jason straightened. "Seriously?"

"Yep. Wants to exit by summer. You up for a trip?"

"Always."

He ended the call and stared at the wall calendar. Two years since he signed the contract that made him CEO. Two years since the blink of a cursor had changed everything.

Now the real game, the industry roll-up, was about to begin.

The Texas sun hit like a furnace the morning they toured the distribution company's moderate-sized warehouse. Jason walked beside Don and Chester, notebook in hand, sweat running down his collar.

The operation was clean, efficient, profitable. The owner, Steve, looked worn but content, like a man who'd built something solid and was finally ready to rest.

At dinner that night, they talked numbers over chicken-fried steak and pecan pie.

"I want a fair price and a clean break," Steve said.

"We can do that," Don replied. "Jason's the guy who'll keep your legacy intact."

Steve studied Jason. "You the one running the Butler operation?"

"That's me."

"Treat my people right and we've got a deal."

Jason extended a hand. "That's a promise."

Two weeks later, the LOI was signed. Things were moving fast. Steve was serious when he said he wanted out.

Back in Pennsylvania, Jason gathered his leadership team, Tim the Controller, Linda the office manager, and Ray from operations.

"We're officially expanding," he announced. "Sixty-day close on a Texas facility. Fifty percent bigger than us. Tim, you run the integration model. Linda, HR onboarding. Ray, process standardization."

Ray whistled. "No small ask."

Jason grinned. "We don't do small."

They didn't sleep much for the next two months.

When the closing email hit his inbox, **Wire Transfer Complete**, Jason let out a quiet laugh. Jason celebrated alone in his office after everyone left. No big deal. Docusigns and bourbon. It's the way the world was going to work from here on out.

He texted Don and Chester:

Congrats! One platform. One acquisition. Two locations now.

Chester replied with a single emoji: 💥

That night Jason and his fiancée celebrated with take-out sushi and Dom Perignon.

She raised her glass and said, "To MJ-1 and the Empire."

"To MJ-1 and the Empire," he echoed.

The next twelve months were chaos disguised as growth.

Jason split his time between Butler, Pennsylvania and Texas. Flights, hotel rooms, endless calls. He hired a VP of Sales to manage the southern team and promoted Ray to Director of Operations.

Margins improved. Revenue jumped. The board was ecstatic.

One Thursday evening, Jason got a call. After two hours, he hung up and labeled a new file: **MJ-2.**

"Alabama," he said simply, when he called Don and Chester the next morning. "Family-owned distributor. Third generation. Guy's name is Robert. Ready to sell. Heard we're buying."

There was a pause on the other end of the line. "You're serious?" Don asked.

"Very. Fills a geographic gap. Let's move fast."

They did. Three weeks later, another LOI. Then, complications with insurance that slowed the project down. Jason was obsessed until the issue was solved, convinced that delivering this deal would prove he could handle the pace he had set for himself. Sixty days after that, another *Wire Transfer Complete*.

Three locations. Three distribution deals. Seventy-five employees. Revenue pushing forty-five million.

Jason barely slept, but he didn't care. The high was addictive.

During a late-night call, Chester joked, "You're chasing deals like an adrenaline junkie."

Jason laughed. "You say that like it's a bad thing."

"Just don't forget to breathe."

"I'll breathe after the exit."

The Butler office buzzed with quiet confidence. The sticky note beside his computer showed a single phrase: *Vertical Integration = Legacy.*

Two months later, one of their major suppliers and a family-owned business out of Tennessee, Atlas Manufacturing, became Jason's next target. Buy it, control the supply chain, increase the exit multiple.

He flew down under the guise of striking a deal on a new product line and met with Richard, the owner, a man in his mid-sixties, with calloused hands and a proud smile. They'd done new product deals together in the past, but this time, when they toured the plant Jason saw everything through a different lens.

Machines roared. Sparks flew. The air smelled like hot metal and old oil. This could be the ticket to his vertical integration strategy. He noted every detail as they casually walked the manufacturing floor.

Over dinner, Richard surprisingly confided, "My daughter Karen loves the design side of the business but hates operations. She's not sure she wants this life."

"You're thinking of selling?" Jason couldn't believe what he was hearing.

"I'm tired." Richard said. "I've been at this for a long time. But Karen doesn't want to hear anything about me retiring. She doesn't want me to sell because she thinks she'd lose her job. She loves it here"

"What if she didn't have to get a different job?" Jason said. "She could stay on for product development. If we were your buyer, we'd handle manufacturing and logistics and she could be the head of new product design."

Richard blinked. "You'd do that?"

"Absolutely. We want her brain, not her burnout."

By the time dessert arrived, Richard looked ten years younger. "Let me talk to her," he said. "If she's on board, you've got a deal."

Jason flew home on fire. This was it. The move that would make Crestline unstoppable. And he was at the center of it all.

Then silence. A week passed. Two. Nothing.

Jason called, emailed, even offered another trip down. Nothing.

During a board meeting Zoom call, Don finally said what Jason dreaded hearing. "If this doesn't move in thirty days, we walk."

"She's just scared," Jason argued. "I can get her there."

"Maybe," Chester said. "But we can't wait forever."

Jason ended the call and sat in the darkened conference room, screen glowing with half-finished spreadsheets.

He'd built everything on momentum. Motion was his oxygen. Now the air felt thin.

He opened his laptop and drafted an email to Karen. It had a careful, respectful, human tone.

We believe in what your father built. We want to build on it, not erase it.

He read it twice before hitting send.

Then he poured a bourbon and stared at his reflection in the office window.

Three years since he'd signed that first contract. Three companies acquired. One more and they'd hit the magic multiple.

Millions of dollars in his pocket if everything clicked. He smiled faintly, though it didn't reach his eyes.

"Almost there," he whispered.

Outside, a snowplow scraped the empty street. Jason watched the flakes swirl in the orange glow of the parking-lot lights.

Tomorrow, he'd call again. Push harder. Keep the wheel turning.

He wasn't about to stop now. Not when the finish line was this close.

Chapter Three
DEAL FEVER

Although the conversation with Atlas Manufacturing had gone radio silent, Jason pressed on.

"Don, it's Jason. I just got off the phone with George, the distributor I mentioned last week. He wants us to make a Florida visit. Soon. He's hungry for a deal."

A beat of silence, then Chester's voice warmed. "That's good news. Send over a couple dates. Geography lines up, and the vertical integration story gets a new chapter if the bones are solid."

Jason rubbed his forehead, grabbed an aspirin bottle, and smiled into the empty office. "He sounded tired. The Pandemic took it out of him. He is ready."

"Then let's be ready too," Chester said. "I'll loop Don in. Book the flights. Any word from Atlas?"

Jason paused, then said, "Still working on it, Chester."

He hung up and stared at the wall calendar. The squares were packed with acronyms and initials, arrows between cities, circles around bank calls. And in one small corner: **MJ-1, MJ-2, and MJ-3?**

Acquisition had a taste now. Metallic, like the tang of a coin on the tongue. He did not name it. He did not have to.

He opened a new folder and typed two lines.

Florida. **MJ-3**.

He shut the laptop and headed for home.

Two weeks later, they were wheels down under a blue Florida sky that made the rental lot look like a car commercial. Don complained about the humidity, then about the car, then about the hotel coffee before it even happened. Chester said it was fine. Jason said nothing. He was already building the dinner conversation in his head.

By late afternoon they were in the lobby, jackets slung over forearms, that pre-meeting emptiness in the stomach that always felt like a knife landing on its edge.

"What did he pick for dinner?" Don asked.

Jason cleared his throat. "The Southern BBQ House."

Don stopped reading the ragged magazine he'd picked up from the side table. "You are not serious."

"His choice," Jason said. "We can eat again tomorrow."

Chester grinned. "We can always eat again tomorrow."

Don just grunted.

The Southern BBQ House was loud in the way chain restaurants were engineered to be. Boiled peanuts. Neon. A line dance erupted two aisles over. The three of them slid into a booth with seats polished by thousands of customers who had already had meetings here, made deals, and left tips.

George arrived in a golf shirt and the posture of a man who had carried something heavy for a long time and had not decided whether to set it down.

"Appreciate you making the trip," he said, shaking hands all around. "Wasn't sure what the dress code is for a meeting like this."

"Jeans and a calculator," Chester said. "We like simple."

Beer came. The room softened.

"Tell me how this goes," George said. "I built a warehouse

and kept it from burning down, but I have not sold a company before."

Don leaned forward, elbows on the table, a smile that looked like trust. "We keep it straightforward. NDA first. You send us three years of financials. We give you an offer we can live with. We do tight due diligence with a team that knows what to look for. Then we close in sixty days. No games."

"Good deals leave both sides a little unhappy," Chester added, almost like an apology. "If one side is grinning too big, we missed something."

It was a line that worked because it was true. Jason watched George's face carefully. The lines at the corners of his mouth softened. His jaw unclenched a notch.

They talked about square footage and racking heights, 5S boards and pick paths, and why Florida drivers could read route sheets without GPS because they had built the routes by hand from the inside out. They talked about inventory buffers in hurricane season. They talked about the year no one expected. About masks and tape on floors and pallets that should have been empty by July but were still stacked in September because nothing moved the way it should.

When the check came, George did not reach for it. He reached for his glass of water instead. The move was slow enough to be choreography. Jason slid the leather book off the table with a practiced hand. Don's smile didn't change, but his eyes said a sentence you did not repeat in public.

Out in the parking lot, Don let it out anyway. "He drags us to a chain and can't move a hand toward a wallet."

Jason shrugged. "He's tired."

"Good," Chester said. "Tired men close deals."

They toured on Saturday to avoid the workforce. The air inside the warehouse was cool enough to fog Jason's glasses for a second. The space was clean. Aisles were marked. Workstations were square and labeled. Racks climbed higher than what Jason had at Butler. He looked up and felt it in his knees. Someone had taught a team to put things in the same place every time. That kind of discipline wrote margin into a P&L.

"Ops guy loves 5S," George said, almost apologetic. "I used to think it was paint and pep talks. The year the world shut down, it saved our backside."

Jason nodded. "It usually does."

They hung at the loading dock and asked the questions that mattered. How often did trucks leave less than full. Who called customers first. What got counted by hand. Which vendors slid invoices in late. Steve answered without flinching. He knew his house. He just did not want to live in it anymore.

Outside, the sun burned white. Jason squinted into it and thought about the template sitting on his laptop. The acquisition model was not a guess. It was a story he knew how to tell, one line at a time.

Back in Butler, Jason closed his office door and spent three hours with Tim on Zoom, refining a version of the truth that would stand up to lawyers and bankers without losing the shape of the actual business. The offer number the model produced landed with a weight that felt right in his chest.

He sent the Letter of Intent with a subject line that did not try to be clever.

Offer enclosed.

George replied the same day.

Deal. I will take it.

Jason blinked once, then walked down the hall to the break room and filled a paper cup with water he gulped down. He called Chester, who put the call on speaker.

"George took the deal," he said.

A second of dead air, then Don's voice in the background. "We should have offered less."

Chester laughed. "Or we got it right. Start due diligence."

Jason hung up and stared at the cup until he crushed it and tossed it in the trash.

A twenty-five percent raise showed up in the first revision of the comp schedule. Chester framed it like an aside. "You earned it. Scale is not a volunteer sport."

Jason said thank you and closed his laptop. Alone in the quiet he allowed himself a single thought that sounded like a bell struck once in a big room.

Keep going.

The due diligence rhythm fit him like a suit tailored by someone with a meticulous eye. The accounting firm was their usual crew. Sharp enough to be annoying, thorough enough to save you from yourself. The law firm had a partner with a voice like a judge and a junior who ran the checklist like a metronome. Jason slept less and did not notice. The check boxes on the shared drive filled, turned green, evaporated from the list.

He made time to learn the names. The ops manager who had taped 5S boards with blue painter's tape on a Sunday and told no one. The payroll clerk who had kept track of shifts on sticky notes until someone bought software. The driver who knew which customer's fence scraped mirrors and who never complained as long as you asked about his old dog first.

Closing came in an email at 2:41 p.m. on a Thursday.

Wire received. Transaction complete.

Jason texted Don and Chester a single line.

Congrats! I heard. MJ-3. Done. Next? 😊

Chester replied with a small explosion emoji. He would have said it out loud if they had been in the same room. Jason allowed himself a smile that belonged only to him, then opened another meeting link and did not mention champagne. The process was teaching him how to celebrate. You clicked the next link. You bought takeout with someone you loved.

That night his fiancée read the number on the screen and whistled under her breath. "To the Empire," she said, clinking her glass to his.

"To the Empire," he answered. The word felt silly in his mouth and exactly right.

Three weeks later, **MJ-3** George called from Florida with a voice that sounded like someone who had put a heavy box down and kept a lighter one to carry.

"You paying finders' fees?" he asked.

"We follow the Lehman scale," Don said on speaker. "You have someone in mind?"

"Friend of mine, a couple of hours south of me. Bigger than us. Fourth largest in our space. They are tired too."

Jason wrote **MJ-4** on his pad and drew a box around it. He worked the phones the way he had learned to work a room. Jake, the founder of one of the biggest distributors in their niche, picked up with the lazy ease of someone whose phone mostly brought him good news.

"Jason," Jake said. "How are you? I just finished a project at the lake. Cannot wait to get out on the water more."

"Sounds like you're building yourself an exit runway," Jason said. "Ever think about what is at the end of it?"

Jake laughed. "Every day. I have a team running the shop. I come in Mondays. The rest of the week I practice retirement."

"If the number is right," Jason said, "you could stop practicing."

"Send me a date," Jake said. "We can talk."

A week of calls turned into an NDA then turned into numbers. Seasonality meant no one wanted to close when the world turned holiday and freight turned weird. They aimed for January.

Jason caught his reflection in a dark window at the office and saw the face of a man who believed his own plan. He did not mind that at all. He wanted to run a lap around the office and also nap in his chair. Instead, he texted Chester and Don.

***MJ-4** is happening. We have a shot.*

Don called immediately. "Then we stack the deck. You are running three sites now. You are about to integrate two more. We need a true CFO. We need a number two who lives in operations. And the ERP you installed when this was one building will not carry five. Get me a plan."

Jason was already writing names. He wanted a CFO who could sniff out a bad accrual in a crowded room and who did not panic when a bank asked tough questions. For operations he wanted someone who loved clipboards and people in the same way, who understood that standard work was not a spreadsheet but a relationship. He sketched boxes on the whiteboard and wrote three words across the top.

People. Clarity. Focus.

He had written them before.

They were still true.

He made a list:

Platform Company: Crestline Distribution

MJ-1: Steve – Texas – Distribution

MJ-2: Robert – Alabama – Distribution

MJ-3: George – Florida - Distribution

MJ-4: Jake (referred by George) – Florida – Distribution

MJ-5?: Richard/Karen – Atlas Manufacturing - Tennessee

The next trip to Atlas Manufacturing to see Richard and his daughter Karen in Tennessee had a different flavor this time. The place felt older the second they pulled into the lot. The main building wore its years honestly. The sign out front was a name that had mattered to good people for decades. Inside, the conference room was functional. The chairs were heavy. The table had nicks like a workbench. Jason liked it. You could set a real tool on this table without an apology.

Atlas Manufacturing was a supplier to Crestline, but now they looked at each other differently. Richard had opened the conversation about being acquired during Jason's last visit, and despite ghosting Jason for a few months, had suddenly invited him back. Don and Chester were invited, too.

Crestline Distribution was finalizing a contract on the new product line and that required the 'big guns' presence. At least that's what the storyline was.

"Congratulations on your deal with George," Richard said as they met in the conference room. "I respect him. He built something real. His dad too. They were good businessmen. Treated their employees like family."

"We intend to protect what they built and make it bigger," Don said.

"That the plan?" Richard directed his question to Don and Chester. "You fellas buy only distributors, or would you buy a manufacturing plant?"

"We buy good businesses," Don said. "Manufacturing is a specialty of ours."

Jason watched as Karen joined the meeting. She had the posture of someone who had learned to lean in even when she wanted to lean back. Her smile was professional. She'd heard her dad's question and her eyebrows shot up. The surprise made sense to Jason. Family companies were always a set of overlapping Venn diagrams. Ownership, management, identity. Pull one circle and see what moves.

They toured the floor and Karen's voice warmed when they stopped by the design area. Walls with sketches. Samples on racks. A prototype in a corner with notes in two different colors.

On the production line, the equipment functioned, but Jason

could hear age in the pitch of a few motors. Maintenance logs showed care and improvisation. He had seen worse. He had seen better. The thing he could not see was stamina. The place needed a new spine.

Back in the conference room, Richard asked the question without ceremony. "You boys serious about buying a maker, not just a mover?"

"We are," Chester said. Don nodded.

Jason turned to Karen. "And we would want you steady in your position. Wherever that is most powerful for you."

She narrowed her eyes at him, then smiled like someone who found that sentence interesting. "I like design," she said. "Operations make my teeth grind."

"Then perhaps you design," Jason said. "And we bring help to the rest."

It was not a close. It was an opening. The meeting ended with coffee in paper cups and the sense that something had started or almost started or could start again if handled with care.

On the flight home Jason drafted an email to Karen that read like a person, not a buyer. He never mentioned that her dad had ghosted him months back but asked about the prototype instead. He asked whether she liked early morning light in the design room or if the afternoon sun helped more. He offered a visit that was not a tour with clipboards, but a day of whiteboards to talk about the shape of the work after a deal.

Her reply came with a smile you could hear.

A visit to Tennessee next week could be helpful.

He booked a hotel with a view of a lake and a restaurant with fish that tasted like it had been in the water before lunch. When she arrived, she was casually dressed, and he stood when she approached the table the way his mother had told him to stand for women who had done their work and showed up on time.

"It's stressful even to think about this," she said as soon as the first sip of wine relaxed her shoulders.

"I know," Jason said. "It should be. It's family."

She looked out across the water and then back at him. "We signed the NDA today. We will explore."

Jason did not let himself exhale until the server asked about dessert. They finished with coffee, then he walked her to her car and opened the door just like his mother had taught him.

"Thanks for hearing me out tonight. There's so much to consider. Perhaps we could continue the conversation, the next time you're in town."

"That makes sense," he said. "I'll have my team follow up with the next steps."

"Good," she said, checking her watch. "I need to head home."

On his way back to his hotel Jason hoped he had done enough to settle Karen's concerns. That she was satisfied they were the best option to implement her father's plans for retirement and equally support how she would like to take the business forward.

The next day he walked with her through the Tennessee manufacturing plant. He could tell she was proud of the business her father had built. Her demeanor was professional as always as she noticed small things. The clean line where blue tape met concrete around a work cell. The sign-out sheet taped to a cabinet door. Small things that bothered her. She wanted perfection in her world. He could see it.

They spent two hours in a small conference room with a whiteboard and a bag of dry-erase markers that barely worked. He drew boxes. She erased one and moved it to a better place. They laughed at a bad arrow. They did not talk about price. They talked about where the people would sit and who would say good morning to whom and what kind of meeting needed to happen on Tuesdays so that Fridays did not feel like a cliff.

When he left to return to the hotel, she walked him to his rental car and thanked him. He still couldn't read her and wondered whether he was at least one step closer to finalizing the deal.

Back at the Butler office he opened his computer and added a folder titled ATLAS. He wrote three lines at the top of a fresh document.

Vertical integration.

Margin.

MJ-5?

He closed the workbook and stared at the ceiling. The lights hummed in the way old ballasts hum. He could feel the number that would change his life sitting behind the other numbers like a picture behind a curtain. In his mind it was a trophy he could grab and touch. It was so close to being real.

November came with cold mornings and sharp afternoons. Two and a half years since the first DocuSign. Jason was not a junior anything. Deals were done, under LOI, or in the queue for closing. The cadence felt right.

Platform Company: Crestline Distribution

MJ-1: Texas Distributor – Steve – Completed

MJ-2: Alabama Distributor – Robert - Fast Close after insurance hiccup – 60 days

MJ-3: Florida Distributor – George - Completed

MJ-4: Florida Distributor – Jake – Referred by George – Finalized in January?

MJ-5: Atlas Manufacturing – Richard, daughter Karen – pending?

The plan felt possible. The bank liked the plan. The board liked the acquisition story. His team had started to look like a team he would have hired if he had been allowed to imagine this.

At night he ran along the river and let his head empty out in a way that didn't feel like rest but passed for it. He texted his boys from the sidewalk outside his building. He put a checkbox next to Orthodontist on Tuesday. He fell asleep with an email half-written and woke at 4 a.m. with the sentence finished in his head.

He kept a small notebook by the bed again. A journal full of dreams and reminders of school visits and his sons' soccer games. He spent weekends with his fiancée.

He felt righteous and tired and right.

He called Atlas Manufacturing to chat with Karen once a week. Not so often that it felt like pressure, not so rarely that it felt like he had forgotten she was a person. They talked about good problems. A supplier who needed different payment terms. A machine that needed a part they couldn't get this month. Whether a color on a label read more expensive if you tilted it under the light.

Some mornings he looked at the bank slides and thought about exit multiples with the clear joy of a boy doing math he liked. Some afternoons he looked at the same slides and felt a wave of something that was not panic and not humility and not fear either. It was the sense that things were balanced on something narrow and that he knew how to walk on narrow things and that one day he might still miss.

He wrote one more word under the three lines on the ATLAS tab.

Discipline.

If they closed MJ-4, the deal with Jake in Florida, in January and the Atlas plant before summer and if the systems held and the people stayed and the market did not punish them for being prepared, then the number at the end was not a number he said out loud. It was a number you did not put in a text. It was a number you honored by not talking about it and by showing up on time the next morning.

He poured one bourbon at his fiancée's apartment that night

and drank it straight down, then poured another. She asked if he was going to drink it. He said he was thinking. She kissed his cheek and left him to it. He drank half and poured the rest in the sink.

When he fell asleep, he dreamed that he was running on the line between two loading docks and couldn't tell which one was higher. He stumbled over boxes and got tangled on the conveyor belt and then was thrown on the floor.

In the morning, he bought donuts for the warehouse because he hadn't done that in a while. He stood in the breakroom and watched a driver take two, then put one back. The small decision told him more about their culture than any corporate report. He wrote Thank you on the whiteboard in block letters and underlined it.

Ray walked in from the plant and nodded at the board. "You getting soft on me, boss?"

"Never," Jason said. "Tell everyone there is a team huddle at ten. We have a lot to do."

Ray grinned. "We always do."

Jason looked out at the floor. Racks. Lifts. Lanes. People. The shape of a company changes when you draw new lines on paper, but you still have to carry boxes. He liked that about this life. He liked that even on days when he loved the math more than moving boxes.

He thought about the email he would send Karen on Monday. He thought about the number he would not write. He thought about twenty-three on the back of a jersey and why it was a good year to stop being polite about winning. He thought about what happens when fever burns off. Then he rolled up his sleeves and walked to the warehouse.

Chapter Four

MORE SHELF SPACE

Jason walked into the office Monday morning with an energy he hadn't felt in weeks.

He dropped his bag by the desk, loosened his jacket, and scanned the small pile of mail waiting on the conference table. Most of it was junk: vendor catalogs, trade magazines, a few envelopes from the bank. Then he saw the box: six inches square, heavy enough to feel important.

Sara, the office manager, appeared in the doorway with her usual morning grin. "Welcome back, boss. How was your weekend?"

"Productive," Jason said. "The acquisitions are going well. Team's adapting faster than I expected."

She pointed to the box. "Someone sent you a present?"

"Apparently. Let's see what Chester's cooked up now."

He slit the tape with his car key and pulled back the flaps. Inside, wrapped in tissue, was a clear resin block about five inches tall, four wide, engraved with the logo of **Crestline**, **MJ-1**, the bank name, and of course **AFPE**. Embedded in the center, floating like a fossil, was a miniature version of their best-selling product.

Jason laughed under his breath. "My first tombstone."

Sara peered over his shoulder. "That's what they call those things?"

"Yeah. The private equity version of hunting trophies."

He set it on the shelf above his desk. The resin caught the light from the window, throwing a prism across the wall. "Guess I'll need a bigger shelf soon."

Sara laughed. "That's a good problem to have."

It was. And for the first time in a long while, the problem felt earned.

The rest of the week blurred with interviews and background checks. The search for a Chief Financial Officer had stretched for months; Chester kept saying, *hire slow, fire fast.* Jason had learned to translate that as *don't screw it up.*

John Reynolds checked every box. He was a certified accountant, had an MBA, and knew how to help companies grow fast through buying others. He understood deals inside out and stayed steady even when everyone else was running on adrenaline. Experience with PE-backed roll-ups. M&A fluency. Calm in a room full of adrenaline. Jason liked him immediately.

They met at a coffee shop near the highway. Neutral ground where no one from the office could wander by. John arrived exactly on time, binder under one arm, notepad in hand.

"I read through the deck you sent," John said. "The pace you're keeping is impressive. Four sites, one ERP, and one more LOI in play?"

Jason nodded. "We move fast. Sometimes it goes too fast. I need someone who can be the brakes without killing the engine."

John smiled, unbothered. "Then we'll get along fine."

By the time they shook hands, Jason knew he'd found his numbers guy.

The next hire was operations.

That one came from a late-night scroll through LinkedIn.

Pete Morgan, former colleague from Horizon Brands, had just posted about "new beginnings" after getting axed in a company-wide lay-off. Jason hadn't talked to him in years. They'd never exactly clicked. But Pete was disciplined, analytical, and unflappable under pressure. Exactly the kind of operator Jason needed now that things were scaling.

He stared at his iPhone for a minute, thumb hovering over the call button. Then he hit it.

"Jason Marchand," Pete said, surprised. "Didn't expect to hear from you."

"Yeah, it's been a minute. Heard about the layoffs. Sorry to see that."

"Thanks, I saw it coming. New CEO wanted a room full of yes-men. I wasn't one."

Jason smiled. "That tracks. Listen, I might have something better for you. You open to a conversation?"

"Always. What's the play?"

"I'm building out the leadership team at Crestline. Platform company. PE-backed. We've got four acquisitions closed, one under an LOI, and we are halfway through installing a new company-wide operating system. I need a new chief operating officer who can build reporting systems, finish the integration, and keep our programmers from wandering off the map. Stock options, fast growth, full autonomy. Interested?"

Pete didn't hesitate. "Sounds like you're describing my next job. Let's meet."

They met for lunch that Friday at a restaurant and found a table in a back corner where they wouldn't be noticed. The small talk lasted exactly five minutes before Jason cut to it.

"Look, Pete, you and I both know our history. Fifteen years at Horizon Brands, and when we did cross paths, it wasn't smooth sailing."

Pete chuckled. "You mean when you'd push for extended credit terms and I'd tell you to get a letter of credit or go home?"

"Exactly that. You were the numbers cop; I was the cowboy. We both did our jobs."

"And fought like hell doing it."

Jason nodded. "I've grown since then. Learned to pick my battles."

"So have I," Pete said. "Besides, I've had worse enemies."

Jason laughed. "That's encouraging."

They finished their burgers and talked about compensation, stocks, and timing. When they shook hands, Jason felt the old tension replaced by something steadier. He thought it was mutual respect, maybe even relief.

"I'll recommend you to the board," Jason said. "They'll want to meet you, but I think you're the guy."

"Then let's win some games," Pete replied.

By mid-November, both hires were official. John slid into the finance seat like he'd always been there, always organized, even-tempered, never too many words. Pete came in hot, exactly as Jason expected. Within a week he'd whipped the offshore programmers into shape, finished integrating the CRM to the ERP and built dashboards that updated in real time.

Jason stopped by his office late one afternoon. "Nice work, Pete. Those reports look sharp."

"Thanks. Still tweaking a few things, but the backlog report is clean. That's the one you said mattered most, right?"

"Absolutely. It's the scoreboard. Last year we found an error late in the season. Our partial orders were still counting full value in the backlog. Could've been a nightmare if we'd missed it."

Pete raised an eyebrow. "Won't happen this year. I've got it coded to roll forward dynamically."

Jason grinned. "That's why I hired you.

Pete smiled back, but Jason caught a flicker of something. Challenge, maybe. Old habits die hard.

December brought the usual frenzy: warehouses humming, sales calls stacked back-to-back, bankers circling for year-end updates. Jason spent most of his days toggling between due diligence for the upcoming deal and keeping Crestline's core business from bursting at the seams.

At night, he checked his phone before bed, waiting for a text from Karen in Tennessee. The vertical-integration deal. The one that would make the whole thing bulletproof.

She was quiet. Too quiet.

He'd already lost a week waiting for her to return an NDA, hers, not theirs, and when the financials finally came, they were incomplete. Two years of P&Ls, nothing else. No balance sheet. No cash-flow statement.

Jason sighed and dialed.

She answered on the third ring. "Hey, Jason. Busy day. Your sales team's killing me. We've got overtime every weekend now."

"Good problem to have," he said.

"Not for my margins."

He smiled into the receiver. "Understood. Listen, I wanted to talk about the financials you sent over."

"Oh. Right. I'm not much of an accountant, so I might not have all the answers."

"That's fine. First question. Any idea why op-ex was so high last year? Revenues were solid, but profit barely moved."

"Oh, that. We bought new CNC and welding machines. Those things cost a fortune."

Jason paused. "So, you expensed them?"

"Uh... what do you mean?"

He heard himself exhale. "Usually those get capitalized. They get spread over a few years instead of all at once. But it's fine.

Probably means what you sent is tax-basis. Maybe easiest thing is to have our accountants connect."

Relief in her voice. "Perfect. I'll set it up."

After they hung up, Jason spun in his chair, gazing out the window. He could still hear Don's voice from their last board call: *If a deal doesn't gain traction fast, it's probably not the one.*

Maybe. But he wasn't ready to walk away. Not yet.

But if Richard and Karen didn't move soon on selling Atlas Manufacturing, he'd move to Plan B. That meant buying their major competitor. Higher risk, bigger retooling costs. He didn't like the math.

The next morning, before heading to his office, Jason walked through the warehouse. Forklifts beeped. Air compressors kicked in. The smell of cardboard and diesel mixed with coffee from the breakroom. The sound reminded him of why he did this. It was the sound of things moving forward.

He stopped by the loading dock where Ray was supervising a new shipment.

"Morning, boss," Ray said. "Backlog is thirty percent above last year."

Jason grinned. "That's what I like to hear."

He walked to his office, checked the time, and realized he still hadn't opened the two boxes that arrived the day before.

The first was small: two floating shelves, walnut finish, for his office wall. He'd been out of room since the Florida tombstone showed up.

The second was bigger. He slit the tape, peeled the cardboard back, and laughed out loud.

A three-by-five poster of Michael Jordan, mid-air, number 23 blazing red against the white Bulls jersey.

Jason unrolled it across the conference table. The paper smelled faintly of ink and memory.

When he was a teenager in France, he'd had that same poster

on his bedroom wall. Way back when he played power forward on the all-state team and believed that discipline could turn into flight. He'd long since given up basketball, but as he gazed at the poster, something in Jason reawakened.

Mounting the poster above the new shelves, he straightened it twice and stepped back. The tombstone caught the light again, the Jordan jersey shining above it like a banner.

"Perfect," he murmured.

Sara passed by the doorway. "Nice addition."

"Motivation," Jason said. "Every dynasty needs a little motivation."

By December's end, the numbers were ridiculous. Sales through the roof. Backlog bursting. Butler humming, Texas maxed out, Florida coming online.

At the quarterly Zoom board call, Chester opened with a grin. "Jason, you're becoming quite the sandbagger."

Jason laughed. "I prefer *realist.* I thought budgeting five-percent growth was aggressive enough."

"Guess not," Don said. "The new marketing campaign's a rocket. You could've doubled that."

John jumped in. "Once we've shipped all the backlog, our trailing-twelve-month earnings will let us change the debt structure for MJ4. Lower cash contribution, take on more financing, and our returns instantly look stronger."

Don's eyes lit up. "Now you're speaking my language. Show me options before Friday's meeting."

Jason sat back, half-listening, half-watching the early snow falling past the conference-room window. The company was winning on every front. He could feel the swell of it. The momentum turning into confidence, confidence turning into something bigger.

"Good work, gentlemen," Chester said, closing his notebook. "One last thing. We've got the Crestline annual fund meeting next month. The partners want to meet the man behind the headlines. You up for a keynote?"

Jason smiled. "Tell me when and where."

That night, after everyone left, Jason stood in his office, lights low, parking lot lights slipping through the blinds. The tombstones gleamed on the shelf beneath Jordan's airborne silhouette.

He thought about the coming year; the pending acquisition, the factory deal that still hung in limbo, the keynote he'd deliver to investors who wanted proof that lightning could strike again.

He poured a bourbon, took one sip, and set it beside the resin block. The reflection of the glass and the trophies merged into something that looked like flame.

He stared at it until the outline blurred.

He'd built the shelf for trophies. He hadn't yet realized he was also building an altar.

Chapter Five

HIGH STAKES, HIGHER PRESSURE

There were bank meetings, and then there were *bank meetings.*

Jason had been in dozens over the years, mostly routine check-ins, quarterly reviews, line-of-credit renewals. But this one was different. When leverage was high and growth depended on borrowed fuel, the energy in the room changed.

He straightened his tie in the car mirror outside AFPE headquarters and watched his reflection steady itself. Inside, the air always smelled faintly of espresso and ambition. The kind of place where every conversation started with *performance* and ended with *risk tolerance.*

He'd spent the weekend polishing the deck of eighteen slides of proof that Crestline's roll-up strategy was working. Revenue projections up two and a half million. Cash flow strong. Margins expanding. After three straight years of beating forecasts, the company had become a bank favorite.

Jason grabbed his laptop and walked in. Showtime.

They took the big conference room. The one with glass walls, too much daylight, the table lined with legal pads and cold-water bottles. Chester opened the meeting with practiced charm. Don played the closer. Jason ran point.

"With sixty days left in the fiscal year," he said, pacing slowly behind his chair, "we're on track to beat our estimates by two and a half million. The team's executing the integration flawlessly. We're requesting a modest expansion of our working-capital line to accommodate the next acquisition."

Nods around the table. Questions came fast on inventory turns, customer concentration, and debt ratios. Jason fielded them like fastballs he'd already seen in warm-up.

Ninety minutes later, the lead banker closed his folder. "Everything looks strong. I'll present to the credit committee next week. You should have a formal approval shortly after."

When the door closed behind them, Jason let his breath out slowly.

Chester clapped his shoulder. "Beautiful work. You make this look easy."

"It isn't," Jason said, smiling. "But it's fun when it works."

They crossed the street to the bourbon bar, a ritual now. Don ordered a Manhattan, Chester went Old Fashioned, and Jason ordered Pappy 20-Year, the bartender raising an eyebrow.

"Cheers, boys," Chester said, raising his glass. "Everything's coming together."

The amber light caught the ice just right, and for a second Jason believed it. For a second, he smiled. A split second of celebration.

The next morning, he was back in the office before eight. Valerie, his sales manager, was already waiting with her laptop open.

"I've got the new sales-progress report ready," she said. "Different segmentation, cleaner visuals."

Jason leaned against the table, scanning the spreadsheet. Something didn't sit right.

"These totals are low by five million," he said.

Valerie frowned. “That can’t be right. The numbers feed straight from the CRM. Live sync to the ERP.”

“In theory, yeah,” Jason said. “But syncs aren’t gospel. I scrubbed the data myself before the bank meeting. We’re five million light here.”

She scrolled fast. “Could be missing territory codes. Maybe the feed skipped records?”

“Let’s test it. Do year-to-date shipments tie to the P&L?”

Valerie clicked through, chewing her lip. “Close. Off by a rounding error or two. Probably uncollectable customer invoices.”

“So, shipments are fine,” Jason said. “Which means the gap is from orders that were received but weren’t fulfilled.”

He paused. “That entire five million shortfall is a backlog of orders!”

A tight silence settled between them. Jason felt the familiar rush of adrenaline turn cold.

No. No, no, no.

He grabbed his phone. “Get John and Pete down here. Now.”

Within minutes, the four of them were in the conference room, laptops open, the air dense with unspoken blame.

“Let’s trace it,” Jason said. “Click a few open orders.”

Pete pulled up the report on the wall monitor. Rows of numbers filled the screen. Columns for customers, ship date, amount, status. Jason’s eyes moved line by line, then stopped.

“There,” he said. “That order shows full value, even though ninety percent shipped last quarter.”

Pete squinted. “That’s not possible. The formula pulls remaining balance.”

Jason clicked into the details. The math didn’t lie. The report was counting original totals, not the unshipped remainder.

He felt heat crawl up his neck.

“You’ve got to be kidding me.”

Pete turned defensive. “We tested the feed last month...”

“Then the test was wrong,” Jason snapped. “We’ve been running forecasts off inflated backlog for ninety days.”

Silence again.

Valerie’s voice was small. “What’s the damage?”

Jason ran the numbers in his head. “We’re not five million ahead of budget. We’re *on* budget.”

John exhaled slowly. “The bank presentation...”

Jason cut him off. “We told them we’d beat the plan by two-and-a-half. Good thing we sandbagged.” He stood, hands on hips, pacing. “Here’s the plan: clear your schedule for tomorrow morning. We rebuild every forecast, including Q4 and next year’s budget. I want revised numbers before lunch.”

He stopped pacing, the anger giving way to calculation. “If we hustle, we can close half that gap. The bank doesn’t need to know we were flying blind.”

He looked at Pete but didn’t trust himself to speak further. The disappointment was heavy, sharper than rage. He stayed silent. Pete avoided his glare, but the moment he stepped out of the conference room, Jason heard a fist slam into the wall followed by a string of expletives.

That night Jason stayed late, the glow of spreadsheets lighting the office like a single bulb in a tunnel. He kept hearing the echo of Chester’s toast: *Everything’s coming together.*

It didn’t feel like it.

At ten-thirty he pushed back from the desk, walked to the window, and stared at the parking-lot lights below. Somewhere between ambition and exhaustion, he whispered to no one, “How the hell did we miss that?”

The answer didn’t matter. The fix did.

By mid-morning the next day, the forecast rebuild was in full swing. The team clustered around monitors, coffee cups multiplying. The new projections brought them back to reality: budget met, not beaten. No disaster, but no victory either.

Just a hairline crack. The kind you only recognize once the whole thing starts to lean.

Jason rubbed his temples. "All right. I'll brief Don and Chester. Better they hear it from me."

He stepped into his office, shut the door, and dialed in.

Chester answered first. "Hey, how's our rock star doing?"

Jason hesitated. "We've got a data-integrity issue. The backlog report overstated open orders. We're still on budget, but not above it."

Don's voice came through, dry. "What happened?"

"Formula error. We're correcting it. Doesn't change the fundamentals."

Chester chuckled. "Well, glad we didn't promise Wall Street."

"Exactly," Jason said. He tried to pivot the tone. "Otherwise, things are strong. We're finalizing diligence on Jake's deal, and I'm still working on Atlas Manufacturing with Karen."

Don snorted. "How's that going? What are those Southerners dragging their feet about this time?

Jason ignored the jab. "They're going slower than I'd like. Karen's nervous."

Chester chimed in with mock teasing. "I thought you had her on board."

Jason winced, even as heat rose in his chest. "She's cautious. I sent her something to help her think through the strategic side."

"Oh yeah?" Don asked. "What'd you send?"

"A book. *The Ride of a Lifetime*. Bob Iger's memoir. You know, the Disney guy. There's a section about when he met Steve Jobs to talk about buying Pixar. Whiteboard session, mutual trust. Thought it might help frame the discussion."

Don grunted approval. Chester added. "Good. Whatever moves the deal forward."

Jason nodded, grateful the conversation could now be moved on.

He cleared his throat. "Speaking of above and beyond... can I ask about comp?"

"Shoot," Don said.

"When we closed the Florida deal, you gave me a bump. With another deal on deck, what's the outlook?"

"Good timing," Chester said. "We built the new model last week. Another twenty-five percent raise."

Jason leaned back, masking the flicker of disappointment. "Appreciate that. I was expecting maybe a little more, given the scale."

"Context, my friend," Don replied. "You started on the low side because the platform was small. With this bump, you're top of range for our CEOs. The rest comes through your stock options. You'll be well in the seven digits when we exit."

Jason smiled into the receiver. "Understood. I'm grateful."

He waited half a beat, then added casually, "There's one small thing that would mean a lot. A new car. Nothing crazy, just an upgrade. Feels like time."

He heard Chester laugh. "You know we're both car guys, right?"

"That's why I'm asking."

Don bit. "What are you thinking?"

"The new BMW M440i. Inline six, zero to sixty under five seconds. Lease is about fifteen hundred a month."

Chester didn't even pause. "Approved."

Jason grinned. "Appreciate it, gentlemen."

When the line clicked dead, he stood in the silence, raised a fist, and whispered, "Yes."

He walked out to the parking lot, breathing the crisp winter air. In two weeks, he'd be signing Jake's deal, driving something that sounded like a jet, and standing in front of the partners as the star CEO in AFPE's portfolio.

Everything was fine.

That's what he kept telling himself as the adrenaline started to fade. *Everything was fine.*

But the truth pressed back. The mis-reported backlog, the missed nights of sleep, the tightening in his chest that came and went like bad weather.

He paused by his car, hand on the door handle, waiting for the knot in his stomach to ease.

It didn't.

He started the engine, the hum filling the quiet, and told himself again what he needed to believe.

Everything's fine. Everything's under control. Everything will work out.

The lie was small. Just big enough to get him through the night. Just big enough to fool his fiancée, and just big enough to keep the walls from caving in.

Chapter Six

CLOSING DEALS, IGNORING SIGNALS

Jason woke before dawn, heart thudding like he'd sprinted in his sleep. The feeling followed him all the way to work. The same dull heaviness he'd had in 2008 when the market collapsed, and every forecast was guesswork.

If you don't deal with reality, it'll deal with you, his old-boss Bob used to say.

Fine. Time to deal.

By the time the team gathered in the conference room, his coffee was already cold. The revised forecasts were on the screen, color-coded optimism fading under fluorescent light.

"We can live with this," Jason said, forcing conviction. "We rebuild, stay focused, and move forward."

Everyone nodded, except Pete. He sat back, arms crossed, jaw set tight.

Jason caught the defensive, brittle look. He, himself, had used that posture before, years ago, back when he was a rising manager clashing with a young A/R clerk who couldn't stand being wrong. Now the roles were reversed.

After the meeting, Jason lingered by the window, phone in hand. He knew who to call. A business coach and colleague he'd known for over a decade.

"Hi, Kate. It's been a while."

"Jason! Good to hear from you. How's life in CEO-land?"

"Fast," he said. "Too fast. I've got a culture issue brewing. My COO's brilliant, but he bulldozes people. Technically solid, emotionally... rough."

"Tell me more."

"He built our systems, kept us on schedule. But he gets defensive and snaps when challenged. I've been ignoring it because he delivers. Recently, he blew a major project and now I can't ignore the problem."

Kate's tone softened. "You can't scale dysfunction. I've been using a seven-week mindfulness and accountability framework with execs who need to reset their habits. Weekly sessions. Want to try it?"

"Do it," Jason said. "Before it gets worse."

Pete agreed to the coaching. To Jason's surprise, he didn't argue. Maybe the timing wasn't too late after all.

Two fires down, one inferno left. The Tennessee deal with owners Richard and Karen had come back to life.

The flight south was uneventful. Jason worked through emails while Pete scrolled through technical specs of Atlas's legacy ERP, the ageing software that ran everything from orders to accounting. By the time they landed, both were half-buzzed on bad coffee and good strategy.

Karen met them at the plant, clipboard in hand, dressed in jeans, boots and a denim jacket. The image of a leader trying to balance grace with grit.

"Morning, gentlemen," she said. "Let's start on the floor."

The air inside was heavy with metal and heat. Machines clanked rhythmically, the smell of welding flux hanging like fog.

Pete leaned close. "That ERP's a dinosaur. Looks like something coded in DOS."

"Keep your voice down," Jason muttered. "Don't call her baby ugly."

Pete smirked. "Noted."

They watched two women babysitting wire spools to keep them from jamming. Pete shook his head. "Five-hundred-dollar sensor would automate that."

"Add it to the list," Jason said.

Karen rejoined them, brushing dust from her sleeve.

"So," Jason asked lightly, "ever consider switching to a more off-the-shelf system? Easier maintenance, better reporting?"

Karen laughed. "We've spent years building this one. With so much invested it'd be a real shame to walk away from it."

Jason nodded, masking his wince. *Sunk costs.* He caught Pete's smirk and forced a smile.

They filled pages of notes, revealing bottlenecks, redundancies, and integration possibilities. The more they saw, the more convinced they became: this company needed rescuing.

By late afternoon, they headed for their next stop. Doug, the company's accounting firm.

Karen bragged about him on the drive. "Doug's a published author," she said proudly. "He wrote a book on valuation they use in college classes."

Jason exchanged a glance with Pete. *Oh boy.*

The CPA firm looked like a set from a Southern courtroom drama: dark paneling, heavy blinds, diplomas crowding the walls. The secretary ushered them into the lobby to wait. When Doug finally emerged, he looked every bit the caricature; suspenders, cuff-monogrammed shirt, booming voice.

"Gentlemen! Come on in."

His office gleamed with polished wood and ego. Miniature models lined the shelves full of cars, planes, even a toy semi-truck.

"See that?" Doug pointed to a sleek model jet on his desk.

"My Embraer Phenom 100. Needs a short runway, perfect for my strip outside town."

Jason nodded politely. Pete kept his poker face.

Doug continued, unstoppable. "And over there. That's my Mercedes-Benz 560 SEC 6.0 AMG Widebody. Rare import. But my favorite's the Mack Truck replica. My dad bought me the real one for my fiftieth."

Jason forced a laugh. "Quite a collection."

"Speed and power," Doug said, settling behind the desk. "Two things you boys seem to like too, right?"

Jason sat forward, tone even. "We like good businesses, Doug. That's why we're here."

The accountant folded his hands. "Let's get to it. You've bought four of Atlas's distributors already. Now you're here to lowball her. I don't think Richard should sell. Karen's talented, and if she needs capital, I can introduce her to *private equity*."

He said the words like they were sacred.

Jason kept his voice calm. "Appreciate the concern, but you've got the wrong picture. We don't strip companies; we build them. The sellers who joined us retired happy, their teams kept intact. Richard himself asked if we'd consider buying a manufacturer. Karen invited us to explore."

Doug leaned back. "Then pay what it's worth to you, not what the numbers say."

Jason caught the opening. "We can't price without data. No investor or bank will. That's why we're here to make sure we're all looking at the same facts."

Doug frowned. Karen sat quietly, hands folded in her lap, eyes darting between them.

"And for the record," Jason added, "Crestline *is* private equity backed. AFPE owns us outright."

The air shifted. Doug's chest deflated just slightly. "Ah. Well. Maybe we can work something out."

"I think so," Jason said. "Karen's done great work. Under our umbrella, she could focus on design and product innovation while we handle the infrastructure. Win-win."

Doug nodded, recalibrating. "I'll have my team pull whatever she approves."

Jason smiled. "Perfect. I'll send the data list today."

They all stood. Doug walked to a cabinet, retrieving two thick books.

"My treat," he said. "Signed copies of my valuation text."

Jason accepted the gift with a tight smile. Later, the second they hit the airport, the books were dumped in the nearest trash can.

They met with Karen for coffee after the meeting, back in her conference room, decompressing over paper cups and soft music.

"So," Pete asked, "how do you think that went?"

Karen shrugged. "Fine, I guess. I'm still learning how this works."

"No worries," Jason said. "First meetings can be posturing. Once we get the numbers, we'll make a fair offer. And remember. You're in control. If you don't like the valuation, you can say no. Or sell part now, keep forty-nine percent, cash out later when we grow it together. Either way, you win."

Karen nodded slowly. "It's a lot to think about. My dad built this place. Hard to imagine letting go."

"I get it," Jason said gently. "You only sell once. We'll make it painless."

They left her with reassurances and smiles. On the way to the airport, Pete exploded.

"Can you believe that guy? Bragging about his damn jet!"

Jason laughed. "Unbelievable. But we got through it. Karen's open. Give it a week and we'll have her numbers."

He texted Don and Chester from the back seat: *Meeting productive. Expecting financials next week.*

Don called within minutes. "Talk to me."

Jason summarized. Don listened, then said flatly, "Red flags. Deals that crawl at the start rarely sprint at the end. Gain speed or die."

Jason glanced at Pete, who was mouthing *ignore him.*

"Understood," Jason said. But inside, a familiar defiance rose.

He'd dismissed Karen's earlier comment about how hard it was for her to let go of the business her dad had built. Sentiment slowed deals. But Karen's accountant was on their side now. Jason could close this one too.

Back in Pennsylvania, the days blurred again with the grind of business. Warehouse issues, forecast reporting, and nonstop calls. They weren't going to recover the full shortfall, but the year would close near target. Good enough for the board, good enough for the bonus grid.

Jason wasn't about to let a decimal ruin his streak.

He had hit maximum payout every year since taking the job, and he wasn't stopping now.

A week went by. No packet from Tennessee. No numbers. Just a short email from Karen that read like a weather report. Busy. Overtime. We will get you what you asked for soon.

Jason stared at the single line and felt his pulse climb. He typed a reply and deleted it. He called, let it ring, but didn't leave a voicemail. He sent the accountant a tightened request list with dates in bold. Then he walked a slow lap through the warehouse to keep from saying something he could not unsay.

Valerie intercepted him at the dock. "Open orders are clean now. The new report is holding."

"Good," he said. "Keep eyes on it twice a day. Morning and midafternoon."

Back in his office he opened the partners keynote outline and tried to write an opening that sounded confident but not cocky. The cursor blinked. He closed the deck and opened the model for the January closings instead. Dates. Cash needs. Day-one tasks. Every box had a checkmark in it.

Near noon, Pete stepped in. “Coaching session one went fine. Kate wants me journaling before morning huddles. I can do that.”

Jason nodded. “Good.”

Pete hesitated. “You heard from Tennessee?”

“Not yet.”

Pete shifted his gaze toward the floor. “I will run the plant equipment requirements the second we get numbers. We can map integration in parallel.”

“Do it,” Jason said. “And, Pete, working with Kate is just one step forward. Chester and Don want more oversight on operations.”

Pete nodded but didn’t push back. Jason waited until the door closed to let his shoulders drop.

By late afternoon he tried Karen again. Straight to voicemail. He typed a different kind of email message. Short. Human.

“Hope the lines are running steady. We can set the call at your pace. Evenings are fine.”

He hit send and watched the screen like it might answer back.

Nothing.

He packed his bag and stopped at the wall on his way out. The tombstone caught the last light from the window. The Jordan poster above it looked almost alive in the dim. For a second he saw the whole hallway of future trophies in his mind. Florida. Texas. Georgia. Tennessee. The acquisition story wrote itself when you stood far enough away.

His chest tightened. A small glitch just under the sternum. He waited for it to pass. It did, slowly.

On the drive home he dictated a list into his phone. Bank follow up. LP rehearsal slots. Cross-site ops cadence. Tennessee escalation plan if no data by Friday. He added a line that did not belong on a business list and left it there anyway. Call doctor back.

Night settled over the townhouse parking lot when he pulled in. He sat in the quiet car a long minute, breath fogging the glass. Then he went upstairs and opened the laptop again. Three deals completed, one hung at 99 percent. One hovered like a promise just out of reach.

He reminded himself that momentum is made, not found.

He reminded himself that he was good at this.

He reminded himself that the feeling in his chest was only fatigue.

He stood and crossed to the window. Streetlights smeared into long lines on the glass. He could see his reflection between them. Tie loosened. Eyes a shade too bright.

"Everything's fine," he said softly.

The room did not argue.

Chapter Seven
EVERYTHING IS FINE

The room exhaled when the Florida acquisition with Jake closed. **MJ-4.** Papers signed, photos taken, champagne poured into plastic flutes. Just as promised in January. On time. On budget.

Jason smiled for the team photo and told himself he should feel proud.

Don called it a textbook close. Chester said, "When both sides walk away a little unhappy, it means you did it right."

Jason laughed with them, but under the noise, his pulse thudded. There was no finish line, only the next race.

Travel came in waves. He'd just finished a two-week circuit visiting all four offices, checking integration plans, meeting warehouse managers, doling out enthusiasm, encouragement, and reassurance behind a tight smile that came from exhaustion and the pressure he refused to name.

Every stop looked the same. Whiteboard. Coffee cups. Exhausted optimism.

He was halfway through his Monday email backlog when Pete appeared at his door.

"Got a minute?"

Jason leaned back. "Always. What's up?"

Pete closed the door. "We've got a truck problem."

Jason blinked. "Define problem."

"You know that nationwide contract kicking off next month in Florida? We planned to rent twenty extra trucks for it."

"Yeah. Logistics mapped. Rates confirmed. What's wrong?"

"There aren't any."

Jason frowned. "Any what?"

"Trucks. None for rent. Anywhere."

"That's not possible."

Pete shrugged. "We called every vendor. They're dry. Global supply-chain hangover from the Pandemic. Chip shortage. Some factory can't finish windshield wiper systems, so whole fleets are parked waiting for parts."

Jason stared at him. "We can't not deliver. What about buying?"

"Dealers have a few. But new prices are up twenty percent, used ones are picked over. I thought we'd grab five or six and keep looking for rentals."

Jason's tone sharpened. "Five or six? We need twenty. I'm not walking into this contract half-ready."

Pete hesitated. "That's two and a half million dollars of metal sitting in the yard."

"Then we buy two and a half million dollars of metal." Jason's voice cracked like a whip. "Remember how Bob used to call this a belt-and-suspenders moment. No risk, no miss."

Pete gave a small nod but didn't look convinced.

Jason turned to his monitor. "I'll loop in John, check the covenants, and let the board know. Order the trucks."

Pete started to say something, then stopped. "You're the boss."

"That's right," Jason muttered.

That night Jason slept three hours. At 3 a.m. sharp his eyes flew open, heart hammering.

Numbers looped through his head: debt to EBITDA ratio, cash flow coverage, payroll. Could the business realistically earn its way out of this? The mental math turned into a catastrophe.

His imagination ran wild. Bank cancels the line. Crestline misses payroll. Headlines. Humiliation.

He sat up, drenched in sweat, whispering into the dark. "Everything is fine. Everything is fine."

The words sounded steady enough to pass for truth.

By sunrise he was on the treadmill downstairs. He ran until thoughts blurred into static.

At work by seven-thirty, he checked his inbox. Still nothing from Tennessee. Three follow-ups. No reply.

He muttered under his breath. "What is wrong with this woman?"

Karen had been chatty once, enthusiastic even. Then she'd gone quiet again, like someone flipping a breaker. He typed a curt message, deleted it, re-wrote it softer, deleted that too.

At nine he called Don and Chester.

"Morning, gentlemen."

"Hey, superstar," Chester said. "Still basking in the glow?"

Jason forced a laugh. "Barely. We've got a sourcing hiccup, we need to buy some trucks, but I'll handle it. Bigger picture is, I think it's time for Plan B regarding Atlas Manufacturing. Karen has ghosted us again. I'm reaching out to Mitch at Premier Manufacturing in Georgia. Enough of this BS."

Don's tone was calm, almost approving. "Do it. If she hasn't engaged by now, she's not going to."

Jason nodded, pacing. "Exactly. I'll visit his plant next week. Quietly."

He hung up and exhaled. Momentum. Finally.

The flight to Premier Manufacturing was late. He didn't care. He was asleep before takeoff, laptop half-open on his chest.

Falling asleep wasn't the problem. Staying asleep was.

Every night at 3 a.m. his mind replayed the same reel. Bank defaults. Phone calls. Faces of board members tightening as numbers dropped on a screen.

He told himself it was normal. Pressure was fuel. He'd run marathons on worse.

By the time he landed in Georgia, he'd already planned the pitch.

Everywhere Jason looked in this industry there were second-generation family businesses with owners happy to cash out, retire, and go boating, golf every day, or take their family on the trip of a lifetime. So, it was no surprise that Atlas's biggest competitor, Mitch from Premier Manufacturing, was more than eager to make time for his yacht.

Mitch met him in the lobby, with an easy smile and a strong handshake. His plant was smaller than Karen's, also cleaner and newer, but still carried the same smell of oil and ambition.

They walked the floor together, steel racks towering overhead. Workers glanced up, curious.

"My son and I have been trying to take this to the next level," Mitch said. "But we're spinning our wheels. He hates it here. Not his future, he tells me. I'd like to retire before this job buries me."

Jason nodded. "You've built something solid here. We can scale it fast. You'd stay on for twelve months during the transition. After that, freedom."

Mitch grinned. "Sounds good. My wife and I bought a yacht last year. Planning to cruise the Intracoastal. Ever done that?"

Jason smiled politely. "Not yet."

He didn't mention that he'd never set foot on a yacht in his life.

By the end of the day, they'd sketched an outline. Jason would price out the machine upgrades; new CNCs, and a powder-coating line to eliminate outside vendors. Integration by spring. Marketing deck ready by summer. Another rush to the finish line. The final checkbox ticked off on the list of acquisitions. **MJ-5.**

On the flight home he stared out the window, doing mental math. Margins. Timeline. Debt load. It all added up if nothing went wrong.

Nothing would go wrong.

He closed his eyes and told himself again, "Everything is fine."

It wasn't.

The nightmares didn't stop. Every night at the same hour. Same sweat-soaked sheets. Same reel of collapse.

His fiancée convinced him to start seeing a therapist and he left the first session with a prescription for anxiety. The pills dulled the noise but also the edge. He felt like a pilot flying with fogged instruments.

Still, the team didn't notice. They called him steady. Driven. Reliable.

Pete reported in one morning, dark circles under his eyes. "Good news. Finally, we got the trucks. Twenty of them. Two point four nine million. Paperwork's moving."

Jason nodded. "Perfect. Let's keep the draw timing tight. The bank won't fund until the titles are in hand."

John added, "It's going to be close on the covenants, but if we hit the forecast, and if nothing else goes wrong, we'll scrape by."

Jason smiled. "Then we'll hit the forecast."

Inside, he heard the echo: *If nothing else goes wrong.*

By March, MJ-4, the Florida deal with Jake was fully integrated. The team gathered in the main conference room, blueprints spread across the table: time to focus on **MJ-5**.

The new VP of manufacturing pointed to the layout. "Powder-coating line goes here. CNCs replace this section. We'll double capacity in six months."

Don nodded over speakerphone. "Looks sharp. We've seen a lot of plant upgrades. This one's clean."

Jason leaned back. "Appreciate it. Once this is live, we move on. With Premier in the fold, we won't need to buy a nut or a bolt from Atlas ever again."

Chester chuckled. "You'll put Richard and Karen out of business."

Jason's grin was thin. "She earned it."

The team laughed. Glasses clinked. Someone suggested a round of Manhattans.

Jason raised his glass. "To **MJ-4** today and **MJ-5** coming soon."

They toasted. He smiled for the room and felt nothing.

Weeks and months blurred. He spent mornings on Zoom calls with the new offices, afternoons reviewing equipment specs, nights catching up on reports he couldn't read straight.

Three a.m. still came like an alarm only he could hear. He'd wake, sit on the edge of the bed, and press his palms together.

"Everything's fine," he'd whisper. The dark never answered.

The deal with Mitch at Premier Manufacturing moved fast. Closing day for **MJ-5** came with rain. Jason arrived at the office early, crisp suit, and tired eyes. Papers were signed. Funds wired. Texts from Don and Chester. Photos snapped for internal announcements.

He sent the purchase orders for the new machines before lunch.

For the first time in months, he felt a flicker of calm.

By afternoon he was in his weekly one-on-one with Pete when the phone rang. A familiar number. Southern area code.

"Sorry, Pete. I have to take this."

He hit accept. "Jason here."

"Hi, Jason. Richard from Atlas Manufacturing. Karen's here with me." The old man's drawl came through thick and unhurried.

"Richard, how are you?"

"Well," Richard said, "not great, if I'm honest."

Jason frowned. "What's wrong?"

"You know us down here in the south. You might think we're slow, but we're not stupid."

Jason sat straighter. "Excuse me?"

"We know you bought a plant, son, one of our competitors. We don't appreciate being lied to."

"Lied to? Richard, come on. You guys were dragging your feet. We figured you weren't ready to sell."

"You made a deal with Premier Manufacturing behind our backs. That's lying where I come from. We're finishing what's on the books for Crestline and that's it. No new orders. We're done with you."

Jason's mouth went dry. "You can't just cut us off!"

"Already did. Goodbye, Jason."

Click.

The line went dead.

Pete watched from across the desk, brow furrowed. Jason's phone was still at his ear, the dial tone humming like static.

He lowered it slowly; eyes fixed on nothing.

Outside, the rain turned to a downpour.

Chapter Eight

IGNITION POINT

Jason sat frozen, the phone against his cheek, rain streaking down the window behind Pete.

Pete leaned forward. "What happened?"

Jason didn't answer. The words hadn't formed yet. He shook his head to clear his mind. "They're cutting us off."

Pete blinked. "Atlas?"

"Yeah." His throat tightened. "Effective now."

The room felt smaller. The fluorescent light buzzed. Pete said something about contingencies, but Jason heard only the slow echo of that Southern drawl. *We're done with you.*

He stood abruptly. "Get the backlog numbers. I want every open order, lead time, anything still in production."

Pete hesitated. "You want to meet with the board first?"

"No. Facts first, board later."

He moved fast, faster than his thoughts could catch him. Action was safer than silence.

They locked themselves in the war room. Whiteboards filled. Coffee cooled untouched. The plant manager, young and unshakable, ran point on production. John handled cash flow. Pete scribbled truck-delivery timelines across the wall.

Jason watched them work, arms crossed, heart steadying by

force. The old Ironman trick. Control your breathing, fake calm until it's real.

"Okay," he said finally. "Phase one: accelerate ramp-up. We focus on core operations, not powder coating. Partner with existing suppliers for finishing. We can sell it later as margin upside for the next investors."

Heads nodded. The plan made sense. So did every plan before it.

For two days they lived on takeout and adrenaline. When the outline finally looked clean enough to present, Jason called AFPE.

Don answered. Chester joined mid-sentence.

Jason kept it clipped. "Atlas Manufacturing is terminating the supply relationship. We're expediting internal production. Cash is tight but manageable. We'll be operational by fall."

Don's tone was measured. "You good? Premier's not teed up until the end of the year."

"We're solid," Jason said. His voice didn't shake. "This is a bump, not a derailment."

He ended the call before the next question could land.

He slept three hours, then flew to Orlando, Florida.

The industry's national trade show and conference was already underway, and his sales team was poolside at a beach resort. Happy hour was starting when he arrived.

"Perfect timing," Pete texted. "They're all here."

Jason stared at his reflection in the elevator mirror. Collar popped, smile ready, eyes bloodshot.

The doors opened to music and laughter. The team scattered in clusters of polos and name tags, drinks sweating in plastic cups.

He gestured for everyone to gather around. "Evening, folks. Good to see you all. Just a few comments."

Conversations dimmed. Faces turned.

"I won't keep you long. Just wanted to say how proud I am to stand here with the best sales team this industry has ever seen."

A few whoops from the back. He smiled, feeding on their noise.

"Tomorrow, we show the industry what's next. You've seen the new line. The 3D-printed, recycled-plastic products. Innovative, sustainable, profitable. And starting later this year, we're fully integrated. No more outside suppliers. Our own plant, our own product. Total control."

Cheers erupted. Glasses raised.

Jason lifted his too. "To the team that made it happen."

He drank. The bourbon burned going down. For a moment the world felt still again.

Later, in his hotel room, he sat on the edge of the bed staring at the carpet pattern until it blurred.

He wondered if he should call Bob, his mentor who had always had his back. He thought of his therapist's advice, who had told him to breathe through anxiety, to focus on something tangible. Then he thought of the marathon training cold-shower trick. Forty-five seconds of pain that forced his mind to quiet.

He turned on the bathroom tap and let icy water sting his wrists. For those brief seconds, nothing else existed.

When he crawled under the sheets, sleep came fast. At 3 a.m., it left just as fast.

Morning brought sun and trade show chaos. Booth setup. Branding banners. Fresh coffee.

Jason walked the floor before the doors opened. Crestline's display gleamed under spotlights: polished steel, bold logos, the future in high definition.

For months he'd pictured this scene. He'd dreamed about the comeback moment. Today it felt staged, like he was watching someone else's victory.

"Jason," a voice said behind him.

He turned. Karen's husband, Chad. Tan, broad-shouldered, confident.

Chad stopped at the display table, tapping one of the 3D-printed samples. "This is trash."

Jason blinked. "What?"

"This stuff? It's made from recycled garbage, right?"

Jason's jaw tightened. "You didn't call it that when you made it. Our new supplier doesn't call it that either. Our customers call it sustainable. Either way, it sells."

Chad smirked. "Guess we'll see."

Jason stepped closer, voice low. "You should head back to your booth before this turns into something you regret."

For a second, neither moved. Then Chad lifted his hands, mock surrender. "All yours, CEO."

Jason watched him walk away, the muscle in his cheek twitching.

Stay cool. Not here. Not now.

The rest of the show was a blur of handshakes, pitches, and forced smiles. Prospects loved the new line. Customers asked for quotes. On paper, it was a win.

By night he felt hollow. He checked his phone compulsively, seeing emails from John about truck titles, from Pete about production delays. Every message, another stone in his gut.

Don't run out of cash. Rule one. He repeated it like a prayer.

When the trade show ended, he went back to Butler and straight to John's office.

"Status?"

John rubbed his eyes. "Still waiting on half the truck titles. Different states, different systems. Once those clear, we can move the debt off the working-capital line. Until then, we're tight."

"How tight?"

"Payroll and plant contractors are fighting for the same dollar."

Jason nodded, jaw locked. "Make it work. No missed checks."

He walked out before the tremor in his hand showed. Everywhere he looked something was burning. Supplier fallout, followed by a cash squeeze and then machine delays.

And still the team believed in him. That was the worst part.

On Friday night he promised himself rest. A long trail run, yoga, quiet. Saturday night dinner with his fiancée. Maybe even sleep.

He got the run accomplished. Not the sleep. His fiancée asked questions that danced around how concerned she was about his mental health.

At dawn on Monday, the anxiety was back, humming beneath his ribs. The shower's cold blast barely cut it. He dressed, poured coffee, opened his laptop, and froze. Fifteen new emails. Same subject line.

Re: Resignation Letter

He scrolled. Names he knew by heart. Half the sales team gone overnight. His chest constricted. The room blurred.

He shouldn't have been surprised. Valerie had told him there was discontent. That many of them were burned out by the constant growth targets. Clearly, bonuses were not enough.

They hadn't said where they were going, but he didn't need a map. Richard, Karen, and Chad had done what he'd once feared. They'd built a new house out of his stolen walls.

Pete found him later, in his office, still staring at the screen.

"What happened?"

Jason pointed. "They quit. Half of them."

Pete read a few lines, cursed softly. "You think she—"

"Of course she did." His voice cracked. "She took them."

He pushed back from the desk and paced. "They were order takers anyway. We'll rebuild. Better ones. Hungry ones."

Valerie, the sales manager, burst into the room. "Want me to prep stay-bonus numbers for the rest?"

"Yeah. RSUs, cash, whatever keeps them here. I'll start calling."

Jason grabbed his phone, dialing the first name. His tone was upbeat, persuasive, borderline manic. *You're valued. We're building something stronger. Don't jump ship now.*

By the tenth call, his voice sounded like static. It had a hollow echo even he could hear.

That night he lay awake, staring at the ceiling. One more day in the office, then Florida again. This time, his middle son's college graduation.

He told himself he should feel happy. He was very proud of his son. So proud, but deep down he was numb.

The next morning, he stood at the whiteboard, marker in hand, trying to rebuild forecasts. Numbers blurred. Columns drifted.

He whispered, "I can't even...think."

The sound startled him. He set the marker down and pressed both palms to his forehead.

A knock on the door. Pete and John stepped in.

"You okay?" John asked.

Jason straightened. "Yeah. Just tired. Need you two to refresh the model while I'm gone. Update assumptions, rebuild P&L. I'll review when I'm back."

"No problem," John said. "Go enjoy the weekend. Spend as much time as you need with your son. It's a big day for him. We got it handled."

Pete added, "Everyone's fired up. We're good here."

Jason smiled faintly. "Appreciate it."

He packed his bag, left them standing there, and called Don and Chester from the car. No answer.

He left a short voicemail for them. "Quick update before I fly. Forecast refresh is in progress. Talk Monday."

When his plane landed, a message waited. Chester's voice: "Call us back."

He did.

"Hey, guys."

"Jason, how are you holding up?"

He exhaled. "Honestly? Not great." The words tumbled out before he could stop them. "I'm sorry, I just...I couldn't focus today. I told John and Pete to finish the model. My brain shut down."

A pause. Then Don's voice, gentler than usual. "You're fine. You made the right call. Let your team handle it. Take a break."

Jason nodded, though they couldn't see him. "Yeah. Thanks."

When the line clicked off, he sat there staring at nothing, tears blurring his vision. The release felt foreign, like his body had made the choice for him.

The weekend passed in snapshots. His son's smile at dinner. The warmth of Florida sun. The click of a camera shutter capturing moments he couldn't fully enter.

He watched everything through blurred vision. Proud but distant. Crushing his son in his arms, fighting back tears, sunglasses hiding his red-rimmed eyes most of the weekend.

His son walked the stage, cap tilted, with diploma in hand. *Outstanding Student.* Three years, full ride offers, law school ahead. Jason clapped with everyone else, smiling on cue. His ex-wife was polite. He was, too. Inside, the noise of his mind drowned out the applause.

The old mantra, "*Everything is fine,*" was gone. In its place: *I can't even.*

At Fort Lauderdale airport, he sat at the gate reading a paperback, anything to quiet the static in his brain. The ending caught him off-guard. It was hopeful, tidy, nothing like real life.

Tears welled before he could stop them. First soft, then unstoppable. He wiped his eyes, looked around, embarrassed.

The tears didn't stop. They deepened, shaking him. Breath hitching. Chest constricting.

He tried to steady it, deep breath, count to ten, but the control was gone. The sobs came harder, spilling over into panic. People pretended not to look.

His phone buzzed. Pete's name on the screen. He answered between ragged breaths.

"Hey, dude," Pete said. "How was your son's graduation?"

Jason tried to speak. "It was great, but..." his voice broke. "I'm not okay. I'm at the airport, and I can't stop crying. I don't know what's happening."

The words dissolved into sound. He hung up before Pete could say a word.

And for the first time since he'd started running this race, he couldn't pretend it was fine.

CRASH AND BURN

The gate agent called for boarding, but Jason couldn't stand.

He kept his head down, breath jerking, knuckles white around the paperback he wasn't reading anymore. Words had turned to water and salt. He tried to steady his breathing. It wouldn't settle.

A mother steered a toddler past. The kid stared, then looked back twice. Jason tried to shape his mouth into a smile. It didn't work.

His phone buzzed. He let it go to voicemail.

He stood slowly, grabbed the armrest for balance, and walked to the restroom. Cold water to wrists, palms, neck. The sting pulled him into the room for a few seconds at a time.

The mirror reflected a man he recognized and yet somehow didn't. Tie loose. Eyes raw. Someone wearing his suit.

He watched as the boarding line grew shorter. His sister, Caroline, picked up on the first ring.

"Jason, what's up? How was graduation? Aren't you so proud?"

His voice cracked as his mouth formed words that came out

in slow-motion shapes and floated across the airport. "Not so good." The phone slipped from his hand and hit the floor. The airline attendant motioned him forward. He was last in line. She stared at him.

"Jason?" Caroline's voice sharpened. "Are you okay?"

He scooped up his phone and scanned his ticket.

"No." His voice cracked. "I'm a mess. Getting on the plane. I'll call you later."

He took the window seat and turned his face to the glass. Not a prayer. A bargain. *Let me get home without breaking again. I'll fix the rest later.*

He slept with his jaw clenched and woke the same.

Morning brought quiet and weight. Sun slid through the blinds. The coffee machine hissed. He watched steam rise and didn't feel different.

The word arrived in his mind as a whisper that grew louder.

Stop.

Not the project. Not the plant. Not the trucks. Him. He had to stop.

He opened his laptop and typed two lines to himself in a blank document.

Can't work. Can't pretend. His hands were steady as he closed the lid.

He answered the phone when his sister called later in the evening. They talked for almost an hour.

Caroline listened. He cried harder than he meant to, said more than he planned. About the graduation. The acquisition pressures. The nights without sleep. The way everything that used to work... didn't.

"What happens next?" she asked.

He wiped his face with his sleeve. Thought like a man who still believed problems responded to rational solutions.

"I talk to Don and Chester," he said. "If I can get two weeks. Just to sleep. Stabilize. I'll be fine."

She didn't argue. That became the plan.

Don and Chester agreed the next morning when he called.

"Two weeks?" Don asked. "Do you think that will do it?"

Jason stared at the wall across from the sofa. "It has to," he said. "I'm not burned out. I'm just... depleted."

Chester cleared his throat. "We can cover the board update. Push the vendor review. Nothing breaks if you're offline for a bit."

"I'll be available," Jason said quickly. "Just not in the office."

"Of course," Don said. "No one's talking about disappearing."

There was a pause.

"Take the time," Don added. "Sleep. Get your feet under you. We'll regroup after."

Jason nodded, hunched over his phone, wiping his face.

"Two weeks," he said again. He needed it to be true.

He made his next call standing at the sink, eyes on the driveway where the car sat clean and useless.

"Good morning, I need to start a disability claim." The sentence came out like he had practiced it. "Severe anxiety. Can't perform my duties."

The woman on the line was kind and systematic. Forms. Doctor's notes. Dates. An email with a link to the insurance policy. Ninety days before benefits start.

He thanked her and hung up. He opened the email. Twenty pages he could not face today.

His jaw tightened. He set the laptop down and pressed both palms on it like a lid. He walked outside, barefoot on cold concrete. The air did what it could.

The first hour filled itself. He wrote a list on a sticky note. *Yoga. Walk. Read for thirty minutes. Eat real food. Call therapist.*

He moved through the check boxes one by one, like the squares could ferry him to nightfall. The mat unrolled. Breath in. Breath out. A small island of quiet.

In the afternoon he read three pages and remembered none of them. Better than zero.

Before dinner he stepped into the shower and turned the handle to cold. Forty-five seconds. He counted. He reached the number he avoided saying, the one that always broke him. He stayed anyway. The cold was simple. He wanted simple.

He slept five hours and woke at three. Not to a nightmare. To absence. The noise returned by four. He walked before dawn on an empty street. The sky, a soft pre-morning blue. The tightness under his ribs loosened a notch.

Back at the table, the list waited. He added one more check box.

Read the policy later.

He stared at that line longer than the others. The ink looked heavier, like it carried more responsibility than the rest combined.

By evening his head throbbed. He lay on the couch with the document open on his phone, scrolling without absorbing, rereading sentences that he couldn't understand. The muscles along his neck went rigid. His lower back ached when he shifted. He slept in fragments.

The next morning, he woke up convinced he had missed something. A clause. A loophole. A sentence that would explain why this was happening to him.

He printed the acquisition model and spread the pages across the dining table. Highlighted sections. Scribbled notes in the margins. Cross-referenced dates with his calendar. Ran numbers in his head until the numbers ran him instead.

Somewhere mid-morning he realized he had been standing

at the table for over an hour, unmoving, palms flat on the papers as if holding them in place.

He sank into the chair and grabbed his laptop.

This was not rest. This was surveillance.

The day passed like that. His fiancée texted endlessly, then called and knocked on the door.

"Door's unlocked," he called, his eyes still on the laptop.

"So," she said. "You need two weeks."

He turned toward her. His eyes were red, unfocused.

"Jason..."

"Two weeks," he said. "I just need sleep. Quiet."

She hesitated, then nodded.

The door closed softly.

By the fifth day, the quiet had become unbearable.

He replayed every decision. The acquisition timeline. The speed. The tone in meetings. The way he had dismissed concerns because they slowed momentum. The look on Richard's face across the table. The way Karen had ghosted him. The words Chad used. The silence that followed.

At night, his mind ran scenarios and audits.

If I had waited.

If I had listened.

If I had pushed harder.

If I had pushed less.

Every path ended in the same place.

He stopped looking at texts. Let emails stack up unopened. Even Pete's updates went unread after the subject line. He told himself he was protecting his recovery. He was really protecting the last thin layer of denial.

At the beginning of week two, Don left a voicemail. Calm.

Professional. Checking in. Chester sent an email. Supportive. Neutral. "Hope you're taking care of yourself."

Jason didn't respond to either.

He told himself silence bought him time. What it actually bought him was isolation.

By Tuesday of the second week, his routines collapsed. Yoga mat stayed rolled. Walks shortened, then disappeared. The list on the table filled with unchecked boxes that felt accusatory.

He stopped the cold showers. Warm water became a compromise. Then a necessity.

Some mornings he didn't get dressed. Some days he couldn't stop crying. Other days he was completely numb, his brain void of thoughts.

The spiral wasn't loud. It was methodical.

He opened old presentation decks and stared at projections that now looked delusional. The MJ Acquisition 5-Year Exit. The number circled in red from a meeting that felt like another lifetime. He recalculated scenarios with different assumptions, trying to math his way back into legitimacy.

The numbers did not redeem him.

He watched interviews of himself online. Panels at industry conferences. Podcasts on successful acquisitions. Confident statements delivered by a man who looked like him and felt like a stranger.

He stared at pictures of his fiancée on his phone, texting one where they were arm in arm, smiling at each other. It felt foreign to him, so he added *Sorry* to the text. Then next: *Thanks for hanging in there with me.*

Her reply came back immediately. *Of course. I love you. Whatever it takes.*

One afternoon he laughed. Not because anything was funny, but because the situation finally broke through him.

He shut the laptop and pressed his fists into his eyes until the pressure hurt. The tears escaped anyway.

He did not get better. He got quieter. He lost track of time and days and stared at a calendar that offered no direction.

On the Friday of week two, his longtime friend Sebastian texted. Jason almost ignored it.

Lunch today? Haven't seen you in a while.

Jason stared at the screen. His first instinct was no. Too exposed. Too raw. But something underneath the instinct stirred. Fatigue, maybe. Or the faint recognition that avoidance had run out of usefulness and he was running out of time.

Okay, he typed. *Noon.*

They met at a place Sebastian chose, casual and unremarkable. Jason arrived early and sat with his back to the wall. When Sebastian walked in, he took one look at him and slowed.

"Hey," Sebastian said gently. "You growing a beard?"

Jason shook his head. He couldn't speak yet.

They ordered. Sebastian talked about neutral things. Traffic. A mutual friend. A new project he wasn't excited about. He waited.

Halfway through the meal, Jason's fork stopped halfway to his mouth.

"I can't fix it," he said.

Sebastian didn't interrupt.

"I keep thinking if I replay it enough, I'll see the move I missed. But there isn't one." His voice cracked. "I built everything on momentum. And when it stopped... so did I."

The words came faster then. The numbers. The acquisition exit. The identity wrapped so tightly around the plan that without it, there was nothing underneath that felt solid.

The two weeks had dragged. Now they were gone.

"I don't know who I am if this fails," he said, his napkin wet from wiping his cheeks. "And I think it already has."

Sebastian pushed his chair back slightly. “You’re not going back to your place alone.”

Jason shook his head weakly. “I’m fine.”

Sebastian stood. “You’re not.”

At Jason’s townhouse, the silence felt heavier than before. Sebastian opened blinds. Made coffee. Stacked papers into neat piles. Jason sat on the couch, shoulders slumped, hands limp between his knees.

“Don and Chester need to see this,” Sebastian said quietly.

Jason flinched. “I can’t do that.”

“I’ll lead. You just have to answer their questions when they come up.”

They set up the Zoom call.

Don joined first. His face softened immediately. Chester followed, posture attentive, eyes sharp but kind.

Jason tried to speak and failed.

Sebastian filled the space. “He’s been spiraling. This isn’t a short-term medical leave situation.”

Don nodded slowly. Chester exhaled through his nose.

“How functional are you right now?” Don asked, carefully.

Jason swallowed. “I’m not.”

Silence.

Chester leaned forward. “We can’t make big moves with you like this,” he said. “And right now, you’re compromised.”

Don continued, “You’ve carried this company on force of will for a long time. That works until it doesn’t.”

Jason stared at the floor.

“We need a plan,” Chester said. “One that protects you and the company.”

They talked about logistics. Interim leadership. Transition terms. It was efficient. Humane. Final.

Jason listened like someone overhearing his own life being dismantled in the next room.

When the call ended, the house felt hollowed out.

Sebastian sat beside him. "You're not your title."

Jason nodded numbly. He did not believe it.

That night, he lay awake staring at the ceiling, the future erased. No office. No exit. No number waiting at the end of endurance. Just morning, loss, and the terrifying feeling of not knowing what came next.

And nothing, this time, to hide behind.

Chapter Ten
AFTER THE FREEFALL

Jason did not wake up panicked about money. That surprised him.

His money was still there, stacked quietly in the accounts where he had always kept it. Bonuses from good years. Conservative choices. A habit of saving that once felt like discipline and now felt almost accidental. He had built a cushion without ever calling it that.

It should have been reassuring. It wasn't. Money answered practical questions. Rent. Groceries. Time.

It did not answer the one question that kept showing up when the house went quiet.

Who am I now?

The days stretched in unfamiliar ways. No calendar pressure. No urgency disguised as importance. Morning came whether he was ready or not. Afternoon followed without asking what he had accomplished.

He tried to give the days shape. Failed. Tried again.

Some mornings he felt almost normal, then felt guilty for it. Other days, the weight of the situation returned without explanation. He'd be halfway through the day when his throat closed and tears came, sudden and uninvited. He stopped trying to diagnose the pattern. Diagnosis was just another form of control.

Sebastian checked in every few days. Brief texts. No fixing. No pep talks.

One afternoon he sent a name instead. *Phillip Remour.*

He works with people after exits. Not performance coaching. Recovery.

Jason stared at the message longer than he meant to. He didn't want recovery framed as a specialty. He didn't want his life reduced to a category.

Still, two days later, he sat in a chair across from a man with kind eyes who did not glance at his watch when Jason spoke slowly. He asked what Jason's days looked like.

Jason told him.

Phillip asked him what he missed most.

He started to answer and stopped. The words he had rehearsed didn't fit. He tried again.

"I miss knowing where I'm supposed to be."

He nodded, as if that made sense. "What do you do when that feeling shows up?" Phillip asked.

"I think about what I should build next."

They let the silence stretch.

"That's not rest," he said gently. "That's substitution."

Jason felt exposed in a way that had nothing to do with vulnerability and everything to do with accuracy.

Phillip gave him instructions. No future planning. No narratives. Track the day as it is.

"What's the goal?" Jason asked.

"There isn't one."

He hated that answer.

Recovery hurt in ways success never had. There were no metrics. No feedback loops. No sense of momentum to borrow confidence from. He kept catching himself trying to optimize his own healing and failing at it. He wanted a deadline.

The old adage, "Failure is not an option," turned out to be a lie. Failing, it turned out, was part of the work.

The news headline in an online industry magazine showed up on a Thursday. He wasn't looking for it. It found him. Forwarded by someone who didn't know what else to say.

Crestline Announces Leadership Transition Amid Strategic Repositioning

That was it.

No context. No arc. No mention of how much ground had been covered before the wheels came off. Just a clean sentence and a quote from the board about continuity.

He read it once. Then again.

The article was short. Other stories waited underneath it.

The company continued. The world moved on. He sat very still. He wasn't criticized in the article. He was erased.

In his next recovery session, Phillip asked him what he felt when he read the article.

"Disposable," he said, surprised by how fast the word came.

He nodded again. No correction. No reassurance.

"That's an honest feeling," he said. "Now tell me what you do with it."

Jason didn't know. That was new, too.

When the pivot came, it didn't arrive as clarity. It arrived as fatigue.

Several months later, a former business contact reached out. A conversation. An idea. A chance to be useful again. A sharp heat flared in his chest. Focus snapped back into place. He felt the old relief of relevance waiting to be reclaimed.

He didn't answer right away.

He noticed that his body wasn't leaning forward. It was bracing.

That night, he didn't rehearse a response. He didn't build a case for why he should or shouldn't engage. He simply let the message sit.

The next morning, he declined. Briefly. Without explanation. Nothing dramatic happened. No collapse. No surge of regret.

Just quiet. He mentioned it in his next session.

Phillip looked at him. "What was that like?"

He shrugged. "It felt small."

"Stay with that."

That evening, he walked without tracking distance. Ate without multitasking. Sat on the couch and let boredom settle without trying to convert it into something useful.

He thought about Crestline and didn't flinch. Not because it didn't matter anymore, but because it no longer defined the next hour.

Later, he stood in his kitchen, hands resting on the counter, and realized something had shifted. Not healed. Not resolved. But steadied.

The freefall had ended. The ground was solid. And for the first time since the crash, he wasn't trying to run from where he landed.

He didn't know what came next. He just knew he could stand here without the need to run.

Chapter Eleven

THE OFFER

Being erased didn't last. Not because it hurt less, but because the world has a short memory and a long appetite for competence. Jason learned this slowly.

First, a text. Then, a forwarded article. A casual, *Saw this and thought of you.* People had noticed the headline. Fewer people cared about the context. Fewer still asked how he was actually doing.

What they wanted was proximity to the version of him they remembered.

He didn't answer most of them. Not out of discipline. Out of instinct.

The quiet had sharpened something in him. He noticed the difference between curiosity and extraction now. Between someone wanting *him* and someone wanting what he could still produce.

The first real offer came on a Tuesday.

Not dramatic. Not even urgent. An email with a soft subject line and a familiar name. A fund he had crossed paths with years earlier. Smart people. Clean reputation. No chaos attached.

He stared at the screen. This was the kind of conversation he used to take while walking through airports, half-present, already anticipating the leverage points. Now his chest tightened.

He waited a full day before replying yes.

The call was smooth. Complimentary. Respectful. They spoke in the shared shorthand of people who had survived rooms where decisions carried weight. The fund partner framed it carefully.

Interim leadership.

Defined timeline.

Stabilization, not scale.

"You wouldn't be rebuilding," the man said. "You'd be guiding."

Jason felt the tug immediately. The old competence lit up like muscle memory. He could see the problems already. The order they would need to be addressed. The calm he would bring by simply entering the room.

It would feel good. That was the danger.

After the call ended, he sat still. Let the afterimage fade. He didn't open a notebook. He didn't sketch scenarios.

He noticed how badly he wanted to be needed again and brought it to his next session.

"They want the version of me that existed before the crash," he said.

Phillip nodded. "And do you still want to be that person?"

The question landed harder than he expected.

"I don't know," he said honestly. "I just know I can do it."

Leaning forward slightly, Phillip said, "Competence isn't the same as readiness."

Jason exhaled. Slowly.

They talked about the difference between leadership as expression and leadership as anesthesia. About how easy it is to confuse usefulness with healing. About how quickly structure can become avoidance.

"What would it cost you?" he asked.

Jason didn't answer right away.

That night, he dreamed of Crestline. Not the chaos, but the early days. Whiteboards. Laughter. The feeling of building something that felt clean and earned.

He woke unsettled.

The next morning, he walked without destination. Let the thoughts come without corralling them into strategy. He passed a café and didn't go in. Passed a park and sat for a while.

He realized something uncomfortable. The offer wasn't wrong. The timing was. He declined that afternoon. Politely. Without a counter. Without leaving the door theatrically open.

The fund partner responded with surprise and restraint. *Any particular reason?*

Jason stared at the question. Then typed the truth.

I'm still learning how to lead without disappearing into it.

He didn't reread the sentence. He sent it. The relief was immediate and disorienting.

Two days later, another temptation arrived. Smaller. Easier. Advisory work. Limited hours. Good money for clean thinking. No operational weight.

This one almost got him.

He talked it through with Sebastian over lunch.

"You don't owe anyone a comeback," Sebastian said, stirring his coffee. "But you do owe yourself a different ending."

Jason nodded.

That night, he made a list for the first time in weeks. Not tasks, but conditions about what leadership would need to look like if it ever returned. What he would no longer trade for momentum. What signals he would listen for before agreeing to step back in.

The list was short.

No urgency theater that would trigger adrenaline.

No identity tied to outcomes.

No role that required self-erasure.

This wasn't a manifesto. It was boundaries.

The week ended quietly. No announcements. No declarations. Just days that held their shape without asking him to perform. He texted his fiancée. *Dinner?*

He didn't feel cured. He felt intact.

For the first time since the crash, leadership wasn't something chasing him. It was something he could choose. And that choice, he suspected, would require more restraint than saying yes ever had.

He looked at the boundary list, then closed the drawer.

Not yet.

Chapter Twelve

BOUNDARIES

Jason didn't go looking for the work. It found him the way reasonable things do. Through a quiet referral. A short email. No urgency in the subject line.

A mid-sized company. One acquisition. Trouble with integration. Smart people who had grown faster than their systems. Not broken. Just strained. They didn't want a CEO. They wanted perspective.

He almost said no on reflex. Read the email twice. Set it aside. Pulled his boundary list from the drawer and laid it on the table, reading it carefully.

No urgency theater that would trigger adrenaline.

No identity tied to outcomes.

No role that required self-erasure.

He checked the proposal against the boundary list.

Defined scope.

Limited hours.

No operational authority.

Clear exit.

He said yes.

The first meeting took place in a windowless conference

room with cafeteria coffee and honest questions. Jason listened more than he spoke. Asked things he used to skip past.

What keeps you up at night that you don't say out loud?

Where do decisions get stuck?

Who pays the emotional tax when speed is rewarded?

The company team wasn't defensive. They were relieved.

By the third session, patterns emerged. Not failures, but habits. Leadership reflexes that had worked until scale exposed their cost. Jason named them carefully. Without judgment. Without drama.

"This isn't about talent," he said at one point. "It's about load."

They nodded. Took notes. Changed small things. What surprised him wasn't how effective he was. It was how intact he stayed.

He didn't replay meetings at night. He didn't track outcomes like proof of worth. When sessions ended, he closed his laptop and went home. Walked the trail. Had dinner with his fiancée.

Leadership without possession. That was new.

The company stabilized. Decisions slowed in the right places and sped up in the ones that mattered. Conflict didn't disappear, but it surfaced earlier. People spoke before resentment calcified.

At the end of the engagement, the founder shook his hand and said, "You didn't fix us. You helped us see ourselves."

Jason drove home and let that sink in. It was the first time leadership felt additive instead of consuming.

He told Sebastian about it over lunch.

"That's what you do now," Sebastian said. "You make things lighter. You help people see what they couldn't see before."

Jason considered that. He didn't argue. They discussed his next opportunity.

A week later, his old coach Kate reached out.

They had crossed paths again at a leadership summit months

before the crash. She was the one who always asked the question that cut through the room.

Her message was simple. *Coffee? I've been following your arc. Curious what you're seeing now.*

They met at a quiet café mid-morning. Neutral ground. No audience.

Kate studied him for a moment before speaking.

"You're different," she said. Not curious, but certain.

"I stopped trying to win," he replied.

She smiled. "That tracks."

They talked about the consulting projects. The opportunities. The boundaries. The relief of being useful without being consumed.

"You know," she said eventually, "what you're describing isn't a career pivot. It's a leadership model most people never articulate."

Jason frowned slightly. "It feels unfinished."

"Of course it does," she said. "You haven't named it yet."

He sipped his coffee. "Named what?"

"The thing you lived through," she said. "And what it taught you."

He felt the old resistance rise. Not fear. Reluctance. The instinct to keep moving instead of looking back.

"I'm not interested in a comeback story," he said.

Kate nodded. "Good. Neither am I."

She leaned in just enough to signal seriousness.

"I'm interested in the blind spots," she said. "The ones that take people out. The ones no one sees until it's too late."

Jason went still.

She continued. "You've been living inside something most leaders avoid talking about because it threatens their story. And I think there's language missing for it."

He didn't answer right away.

Outside, someone laughed. A cup clinked against a saucer. The world continued.

"What would that look like?" he asked finally.

Kate smiled, slow and knowing. "A conversation first. Then maybe a book. Not advice. Not heroics. A map."

Something inside him opened instead of tightening. Not urgency. Not identity. Curiosity.

He nodded once. "Let's continue the conversation." They stood. Gathered their coats. No commitments made.

As Jason walked to his car, he realized something had shifted again. Not forward. Not back.

Deeper.

This wasn't about returning to leadership. It was about translating it.

And for the first time, he didn't feel erased. He felt useful.

Chapter Thirteen

LEADERSHIP AFTER EGO

Jason didn't arrive with answers at their next meeting. That surprised Kate.

Most people who sat across from her at that stage brought conclusions disguised as insight. They wanted to narrate their way out of pain. Jason brought fragments instead.

"Tell me where it broke," she said finally.

Jason stared into his cup. Not searching. Remembering.

"It wasn't one thing," he said. "That's what fooled me. It felt like pressure. Timing. Bad actors. Market noise."

She waited.

"But underneath," he continued, slower now, "there were patterns. Things I couldn't see because the momentum was so strong."

She slid a napkin across the table and placed a pen beside it.

"Show me."

He hesitated, then picked up the pen.

He drew a simple shape. A circle. Labeled it *performance*. Added dollar signs.

"That was the center of everything," he said. "Results made speed feel necessary. Speed made questions feel dangerous. And when questions were dismissed, people stopped asking the ones they needed to."

He added arrows. Loops feeding themselves. Pushing feedback away.

"I thought I was focused," he said. "But I was narrow. I stopped asking questions that didn't produce immediate output."

Kate leaned in, eyes sharp now.

"What else?"

He drew another circle. *Identity*. And added a stick figure.

"I tied my worth to momentum," he said. "Slowing down felt like dying. I couldn't tell the difference between discipline and fear."

His hand moved faster now. Less careful.

Another circle. *Control*. He drew what looked to Kate like handcuffs.

"I believed responsibility meant carrying everything," he said. "Delegation looked like risk. Vulnerability looked like weakness. I trained the organization to depend on me and then wondered why it couldn't move without me."

He sketched some more. The napkin was crowded. Messy. Honest. Kate didn't speak. Jason leaned back and exhaled. His shoulders dropped for the first time in an hour.

"That's the crash," he said quietly. "Not the deal. Not the headlines. It's the blind spots. They stacked. Reinforced each other. And I was rewarded for all of them."

Kate nodded slowly.

Jason smiled faintly. "I didn't lose leadership. I lost illusion."

"Leadership after ego," she said, "Is leadership that can see itself."

He nodded, letting that sink in.

He folded the napkin once. Then again. Not to tidy it. To hold it.

"I thought the crash took everything," he said. "But it took the part that was unsustainable."

Kate studied him. "And what did it leave?"

He didn't answer right away.

"Choice," he said finally. "Boundaries. The ability to lead without disappearing into it."

She smiled. "That's the book."

Jason shook his head slightly. "No. That's the work."

She laughed. "Fair."

She pulled another napkin off the pile and wrote on it. Then handed it to Jason.

Crash and ~~Burn~~ Learn. "That's your title, though, if you do want to write a book."

He smiled and put the napkin in his pocket next to the other one.

Outside, the air had that end-of-day softness. No urgency. No pull toward the next thing.

Kate paused before heading to her car.

"People are going to want formulas," she said. "Steps. Prescriptions."

"They won't get them," Jason said.

"No," she agreed. "They'll get mirrors." They stood there a moment longer, neither of them in a hurry. Then Kate stepped forward and hugged him.

That night, Jason emptied his pockets onto the kitchen counter. Keys. Phone. The napkins. He unfolded them slowly. Smoothed them both flat. The ink had bled in places. Lines crossed where they shouldn't. It wasn't elegant.

It was unfinished, uneven, and accurate. The messiness didn't need to be fixed. It proved he hadn't edited the truth to survive it.

He put the napkins in a drawer, not on the wall. Not as instruction, but as a reminder.

The crash no longer defined him, it had freed him. And now, he would build from what he could see.

He hadn't lost his leadership. He had lost his blindness. That would change everything.

Section 3: Ten Blind Spots that Lead to Burnout

Introduction to the Blind Spots

FROM JASON'S STORY TO THE BLIND SPOTS THAT SHAPE EVERY LEADER

Jason Marchand's crash is not an outlier. It is not a dramatic exception or a rare executive implosion. It is what happens when a leader with talent, drive, and good intentions runs straight into the unseen forces shaping every decision, every habit, and every internal narrative they carry.

Jason didn't burn out because he was weak. He burned out because he was blind.

Blind to the pressure he had normalized for far too long...

To the emotional debts he never stopped accumulating...

To the inner narratives that kept telling him he hadn't earned his seat...

To the subtle patterns he mistook for ambition when they were actually survival strategies...

And to how much he needed from the C-Suite and how little it was ever going to give him.

Here is the uncomfortable truth.

Every leader, even the strongest ones, has blind spots. Not small quirks. Not minor oversights. But deep, structural distortions in how we see ourselves and how we interpret the world around us.

These blind spots become the architecture of our leadership without us realizing they exist. They dictate what we pursue, what we avoid, what we tolerate, and what we miss entirely. They shape our sense of urgency, our emotional reactions, our decision-making patterns, and the way we cope when pressure builds faster than clarity.

Jason paid the price for not seeing his blind spots early enough, and the truth is he wasn't an exception. Most leaders walk straight into the same wall without realizing what they missed.

Blind spots are not inevitable traps. They are simply truths we haven't brought into the light yet. And once you can see them, you can change them. You can correct them. You can build a leadership identity that doesn't collapse under strain.

That is where we're going next.

Because if the first part of this book revealed the five false beliefs that pull leaders toward burnout, then the next part reveals the unseen forces that push them there. These blind spots operate quietly, but the moment you start recognizing them, everything about how you lead begins to shift.

Let's open the door to Section 3 and take a hard, honest look at the blind spots that hold even the most exceptional leaders back.

This is the part Jason wishes he had understood sooner. And the part that will change the way you lead from here forward.

Blind Spot #1:

THE DENIAL TAX - IGNORING EARLY WARNING SIGNALS

Stress doesn't always arrive as panic or crisis. Most of the time, it sneaks in quietly. It builds over months and years, so gradually that by the time you notice its effects, the damage has already begun.

You may even convince yourself that constant tension is normal. It's just part of leading, building, or achieving. But what looks like endurance is often something else entirely: a slow erosion of capacity.

Science has a name for what happens when you live like this.

It's called *allostatic load*: the cumulative burden your body carries when stress becomes chronic. And it can be deadly. Think of it as the physiological equivalent of compound interest. Every time you push through instead of processing, you take out a small loan from your future energy reserves.

Each time you tell yourself, "I'll deal with that later," the balance grows.

Researchers studying burnout have found that people living under long-term strain show measurable differences in their biology. Their cardiovascular systems work harder, immune systems misfire, and their metabolism slows.

It's mental exhaustion, along with physical wear and tear, recorded in the body's chemistry and rhythms.

The most striking part? You don't feel it happening. You just adapt.

The reality is that you're in denial. You're about to pay the Denial Tax.

Two Roads to the Same Destination

The Denial Tax accumulates through two distinct pathways. Both are invisible. Both compound over time. And both lead to the same place: a system pushed past its breaking point.

The first is chronic stress: the relentless daily pressure of leadership. Emails at midnight. Difficult conversations postponed. Weekends that blur into workweeks. This is allostatic load: the slow wearing down of your system through sustained demand without adequate recovery.

The second is incomplete stress cycles: the acute events you never fully processed. These are harder to see because they pose as old news. Meanwhile, your nervous system is still running the tab.

Understanding both requires a quick look at how your stress response was designed to work.

The Stress Cycle: A System Built for a Different Era

Ten thousand years ago, stress had a clear beginning and end.

A hunter-gatherer spots a tiger. The brain immediately signals the release of stress hormones, primarily adrenaline and cortisol. Cortisol prompts the liver to release extra glucose into the bloodstream, ensuring the body has a rapid surge of energy for fight or flight. Heart rate increases, muscles tense, focus sharpens.

Then, one of two things happens: the hunter escapes or becomes dinner.

If he survives, his body receives a clear signal that the threat is over. Hormones return to baseline. The nervous system resets. The stress cycle completes.

That system was perfect for lions. It falls apart in the world of inboxes, investors, and people who need 'just five minutes.'

When the Cycle Never Closes

Modern stressors rarely have a clean finish line.

The deadline passes, but another one is already warming up. The hard conversation happens, but the tension hangs around like fog. The quarter ends, but somehow the expectations reset even higher.

There's no sprint. No physical release. No internal green light telling your system, *You're good. Stand down.*

Because the stress cycle doesn't close, it does something far sneakier.

It **almost** closes. The alarm quiets, but it never fully shuts off.

That's where the two pathways split.

Chronic stress keeps the alarm half-buzzing day after day. Your body adjusts to the hum, convincing you this elevated state is just "how things are now." It's your internal thermostat creeping up degree by degree. Seventy-two. Seventy-four. Seventy-six. Before long, you're living at eighty-five and swearing you're fine.

Incomplete stress cycles from acute events don't work on that slow creep. They hit differently. Every unprocessed stressor, a betrayal you breezed past, a failure you buried, a loss you never let yourself feel, does more than weigh on your day.

It raises the floor you're standing on.

The Ratchet Effect

Picture your stress baseline sitting at a calm, steady 1 out of 10.

Then life throws something sharp at you, a brutal board meeting, a key leader walking out, or a deal you spent months on suddenly cratering. Your stress spikes to a 9. Totally normal.

If you actually processed that event, felt it, named it, let your system come down, you'd settle back at 1. Cycle complete.

But that's usually not what happens.

You *move on.* You tell yourself, "It's fine," and get on the next call because that's what leaders do.

Your body never gets the all-clear. The stress drops... but not all the way. Maybe from 9 to 2.

And 2 quietly becomes the new normal.

Then the next major stressor hits. Same pattern. Another spike, another half-reset. Now your baseline is 3.

Jason didn't notice his baseline climbing. Nothing felt "wrong." He was still performing. Still delivering. Still being trusted with more.

What he lost was resilience and by the time he realized it, resilience was the one thing he couldn't afford to lose.

Repeat that across a career with dozens of crises, betrayals, losses, misses, and pivots, and your baseline creeps up to a 5 or 6 without you even noticing. You're still functioning. You're still hitting targets.

But the ability you had to bounce back? Gone.

A stressor that would've barely fazed you early in your career suddenly feels like a threat. The same level of pressure you used to shrug off now pushes you right to the edge.

That's why burnout feels like it comes out of nowhere. It doesn't.

It's the final straw hitting a system that's been ratcheted tighter for years.

Why High Performers Are Most at Risk

Executives and leaders are especially vulnerable because denial doesn't *feel* like denial. It feels like discipline.

When you push through exhaustion and still deliver, everyone calls it strength. You get rewarded for it and praised for grit, admired for staying calm, and trusted because you always "come through."

That feedback loop is intoxicating. Every win tells you you're built differently. Every crisis you survive reinforces the story that you don't need rest, or space, or help. You just need to dig deeper.

And for a while, that story works. Denial becomes fuel. You borrow energy from tomorrow, and tomorrow always seems to show up.

The problem is the bill always comes due.

Most leaders tell themselves they'll recover later; after the launch, after the quarter, after the next fire is out, after life "settles down."

But life at the top doesn't settle. It stacks until your system can't carry it anymore.

The Collection Notice

The early signs are easy to dismiss. You're sleeping less and waking up tired. You can't remember details. You can't focus like you used to. You snap at people you care about. Maybe your head hurts. Maybe your mind won't shut up long enough for you to rest.

All of it feels like a busy life. But it's more than that. It's your nervous system tapping you on the shoulder, trying to collect on recovery time you never paid.

By the time the cognitive hits show up, mental fog, indecision, the "why did I walk into this room?" moments, the damage isn't theoretical anymore. You've been living in overdraft for years, and now the bill has come due.

The collapse looks different for everyone. For some, it's physical; a heart scare, chronic pain, your immune system waving the white flag. For others, it's emotional; zero motivation, a brain that won't focus, a hollowness you can't explain.

You go from handling everything to handling nothing, and it feels like it happened overnight.

But it never happens overnight. It's the last payment on a debt you've been accumulating slowly, quietly, relentlessly.

The Body Never Forgets

Your body, it turns out, is an impeccable accountant. It doesn't misplace receipts or forget charges.

It keeps track of every moment you told yourself you were fine when you weren't. Every night you traded rest for one more task. The nights on the road when you had one more drink. Or an occasional encounter.

Every acute stressor you refused to process because you didn't have time, or because feeling it would have slowed you down gets put on the list.

The ledger doesn't lie. And when the balance gets too high, the body collects. Sometimes gently. More often not.

I call it the Denial Tax for good reason. It's the cost of convincing yourself that you can outrun biology.

Stress is not free energy. It's borrowed fuel. The adrenaline that powers you through late nights and tough meetings is a loan with interest.

Denial compounds that interest. Each act of avoidance or suppression adds another line to the balance sheet.

Paying Down the Debt

The good news is that repayment doesn't have to be catastrophic.

You can address the chronic stress through boundaries, recovery time, and sustainable rhythms.

You can complete the incomplete stress cycles by finally acknowledging and processing the acute events you've been carrying, sometimes for decades.

The first step is to recognize that both pathways exist. Chronic Stress and Incomplete Stress Cycles. Stress always leaves a residue and our baseline may be higher than you think.

The Denial Tax is not metaphorical. It's physiological. You can pay it gradually, through awareness and intentional work, or all at once when your body demands a reset.

Either way, the bill will come due.

The only question is how much interest you'll owe when it does.

The Diagnostic Chart below will make the invisible visible. It shows the inner mechanics of this blind spot so you can understand not just what you're experiencing, but why your system keeps returning to it.

When you can see the system clearly, your old operating system stops running the show.

Blind Spot #1: The Denial Tax

Element	Description	What It Looks Like in Leadership
Psychology Underneath	Chronic stress becomes normalized; the system adapts to an elevated baseline.	Leaders misread ongoing tension as standard workload and interpret fatigue as lack of discipline.
Internal Pattern that Keeps It Alive	Incomplete stress cycles and constant stress accumulate without true recovery.	Leaders quickly redirect from acute stressors without processing them, maintaining a heightened internal load.
Why Leaders Can't Self-Correct	Denial gets rewarded. Results mask depletion. Push through gets praised.	Leaders view slowing down as loss of momentum and assume they should tolerate more strain.
Underlying Dynamics	Ratchet Effect: each incomplete cycle raises the floor, creating invisible damage.	Underneath a high-functioning facade, a minor stressor can trigger disproportionate collapse.

Blind Spot #2:
THE CONFIDENCE PENDULUM – FROM HUBRIS TO IMPOSTER SYNDROME

There is a pattern I have seen play out in almost every executive I've worked with, and it is one I lived for years without realizing what it was. It is the quiet swing between two identities, both convincing in different ways.

On one side, the voice that insists you are exceptional. On the other, the voice that believes you have no business being in the role at all. Most people think these two states are opposites. Hubris versus impostor syndrome. Overconfidence versus self-doubt. One inflates you. The other shrinks you.

But the research tells a different story. These two experiences are deeply connected and often belong to the same internal system. They rise from the same emotional wiring, the same cognitive distortions, and the same leadership environments that reward certainty while punishing vulnerability.

Executives are not choosing between one or the other. They are swinging between both, often without realizing the movement is happening.

The Hubris Side: When Success Begins to Blind Us

Let's start where most people are reluctant to begin, because hubris feels like an accusation. Yet the data makes something very clear. Hubris is not rare among leaders. It is common enough to be predictable. It shows up as an inflated sense of judgment, exaggerated confidence, and an internal narrative that attributes success almost entirely to one's own brilliance.

And because positional power tends to reinforce this belief, hubris often intensifies the longer someone remains in a leadership role. The CEO title changes how people treat you, how they respond to your ideas, and how willing they are to challenge you. Over time, the deference becomes data. Success becomes evidence. And the internal story becomes, "I am the reason this works."

There is a famous line in management literature that says, 'nothing blinds a leader to the possibility of failure, quite like success.'

It sounds poetic, but the psychology behind it is straightforward. When you succeed repeatedly, your brain begins to over-attribute outcomes to your skill rather than to timing, market conditions, team strength, or luck. Each win strengthens the loop. "I did that" slowly becomes "I can always do that," which can eventually become "I cannot be wrong."

The research shows the consequences clearly. CEOs with high levels of overconfidence tend to pursue riskier acquisitions, overestimate synergies, and overpay for companies. These decisions often look bold from the outside but lack the grounding of calibrated judgment. And the most reliable predictor of this pattern is not intelligence or drive but narcissism.

When a leader starts seeing themselves as uniquely gifted

and internally irreplaceable, their decision-making becomes more fragile and less reality based.

There is a statistic I return to often because it illustrates human bias so simply. Ninety-three percent of American drivers believe they are above average. That number is impossible, and yet it feels intuitively correct when applied to executives. If you asked CEOs how many believe they are in the top half of all CEOs, I suspect the percentage would be very similar.

We know the math. Yet we cannot resist believing we are the exception.

The Impostor Side: When Achievement Feels Like a Setup

Now for the opposite end of the swing. If the hubris state inflates our sense of self, the impostor state compresses it. And here again, the research makes something astonishingly clear.

Impostor syndrome is not a niche issue. Seventy-one percent of U.S. CEOs report feeling it. Seventy-five percent of female executives surveyed say they've experienced it at some point in their careers. Medical residents, high achievers, elite performers across fields report the same pattern.

And then the twist. High performers are more susceptible to impostor syndrome than the average professional. The more capable someone is, the more they tend to question the validity of that capability.

Why does this happen? Because achievement raises expectations. Each success becomes a new baseline, not a celebration. Executives often describe a quiet panic underneath promotions and public recognition. "What if this is the moment they notice I'm not as good as they think?" Instead of building confidence, achievement amplifies the fear of exposure.

Perfectionism plays a major role here. When the only acceptable result is flawless execution, even small mistakes feel like evidence of inadequacy. The pressure builds in silence because the expectations around the role discourage open conversations about doubt. Leaders are supposed to be steady. They are supposed to be certain. They are supposed to know what to do next.

When you cannot admit your internal struggle upward to a board, sideways to your peers, or downstream to your team, the impostor feeling has nowhere to go. So, it grows.

The Pendulum Paradox is in the Swing

The paradox is that many leaders who experience impostor syndrome also harbor private moments of hubris. They can swing from "I'm better than most" to "I'm disappointing everyone" without noticing the shift. Both stories feel honest in the moment. Both are incomplete.

Jason could move between those two stories in a single afternoon. A board meeting where his confidence felt unshakable. A quiet drive home where every decision replayed as evidence he'd missed something obvious. Both versions felt true. Neither felt optional.

The shift is fast. You can go from "I know what I'm doing" to "I have no idea what I'm doing" in a single moment. And again, it will feel honest. It will feel like the more mature, more humble truth. But it is simply the other extreme.

This is what makes the pendulum a blind spot. You cannot see the swing while you are inside it. Overconfidence feels like confidence. Self-doubt feels like realism. In both cases, the distortion goes unnoticed.

The Safe Zone: Where Calibrated Confidence Lives

Healthy leadership does not live at either extreme. It lives in the middle on a narrower band that blends competence with humility and keeps both fear and ego in check. In that space, you can acknowledge that you contributed meaningfully to a success without assigning yourself sole credit. You can admit mistakes without letting them define your identity. You can think clearly without believing you are always right or always wrong.

In that zone, your thinking sounds like this:

I played a role in this outcome, and other factors mattered too.

I don't have all the answers, and I'm capable of figuring them out.

I made mistakes, and I can learn from them.

I'm skilled, and I'm still learning.

This kind of confidence is quieter but far more durable. It does not spike with praise or collapse with criticism. But reaching it requires awareness of the pendulum, and awareness is often the part leaders lack.

Why the Pendulum Fuels Burnout

Both extremes push leaders toward unsustainable behavior, just in different ways. When hubris takes over, leaders overcommit, underestimate risk, and take on initiatives that stretch the organization beyond its capacity. They believe they can handle more than is realistic. They say yes more often than they should. They delegate less than they need to.

When impostor syndrome takes over, leaders overwork, micromanage, and refuse to rest. They fear that any sign of ease will expose them. They demand more from themselves than the role requires. They fixate on flaws, inflate the stakes, and double down on effort to compensate for the internal fear of inadequacy.

The oscillation between these states is exhausting. The internal recalibration, the mental rewriting of "who am I today," drains energy that should be available for decision-making, creativity, relationships, and recovery.

Leaders begin confusing emotional swings with actual insight.

Jason trusted whichever voice was loudest that day. Confidence sounded like clarity. Doubt sounded like rigor. He didn't realize he was recalibrating his decisions based on mood, not information.

That is the danger of this blind spot. Not that the pendulum exists, but that it moves quietly, without your permission, shaping decisions you believe you are making rationally.

The Goal: Reducing the Amplitude

We cannot eliminate the pendulum. It is woven into the human experience. But we can reduce its swing through awareness, honesty, and the systems we build around ourselves.

The goal is to recognize the early signs:

To feel the shift before it becomes an identity.

To pause when confidence turns into certainty.

To breathe when worry turns into inadequacy.

To question the stories that show up at the extremes.

Because when you live closer to the middle, leadership becomes clearer, steadier, and far more sustainable. And the decisions you make, for yourself, for your company, and for the people who rely on you, become grounded in reality rather than distorted by the quiet violence of the swing.

The Diagnostic Chart below breaks down the components of this blind spot so you can understand how it forms,

how it sustains itself, and how it reshapes your sense of self under pressure.

Seeing the system in its entirety helps you recognize the early shifts, before emotion becomes identity, and before the swing transforms into something heavier than it needs to be.

Blind Spot #2: The Confidence Pendulum

Element	Description	What It Looks Like in Leadership
Psychology Underneath	Emotional reactivity to success and failure. Identity tied to performance extremes.	Leaders move from "I've got this" to "I don't belong here" overnight.
Internal Pattern that Keeps It Alive	Perfectionism, comparison, shame spirals, externalized identity.	Decisions shift with mood rather than data.
Why Leaders Can't Self-Correct	Both ends of the swing feel like truth in the moment. Each reinforces the other.	Leaders misread emotional swings as insight instead of distortion.
Underlying Dynamics	Neural sensitivity to praise and criticism, distorted self-appraisal, lack of emotional calibration.	Erratic decision-making, overcorrection, burnout cycles.

Blind Spot #3: THE FOCUS FALLACY – ACTIVITY ≠ STRATEGY

There is a particular kind of focus that executives love to talk about. It shows up in strategy decks, board conversations, annual planning sessions, and every offsite where the team scribbles ideas on whiteboards. But if you listen closely, you start to hear something strange.

Everyone says the word "focus," but very few people mean the same thing when they use it. And even fewer are practicing it.

Most of us think of focus as discipline. Intentionality. Clarity. But real strategic focus is something different. It is more demanding. More inconvenient. More uncomfortable. And it is far easier to pretend you have it than to actually build it.

To understand why, we need to start with what true focus looks like at the organizational level. And then why do so many leaders mistake alignment for focus without ever realizing they've drifted into one of the most destructive blind spots in leadership.

What Real Focus Actually Requires

Michael Porter, who spent decades studying strategy, captured the entire concept in one sentence. "The essence of strategy is choosing what not to do."

It sounds simple until you try to put it into practice. Because choosing what not to do means sacrificing ideas that sound promising. It means letting go of opportunities that could work. It means saying no far more often than you say yes.

And if you're a high performer who thrived by doing more, delivering more, and proving more, this kind of discipline does not come naturally.

The data reinforces this truth. Bain & Company, the global strategy consulting powerhouse, found that eighty percent of sustained value creators were built around a single core business. Companies that succeeded long term didn't diversify endlessly. They didn't try to be everything to everyone. They identified one core identity and concentrated almost everything there.

One business. One direction. One thing that mattered above all.

That level of clarity is rare. And the more success an organization has, the harder it becomes to maintain.

Just look at Apple in 1997. The company was collapsing under the weight of its own complexity. Hundreds of products. No cohesive direction. Steve Jobs walked back in, looked at the sprawling product line, and eliminated seventy percent of it. Entire categories disappeared overnight. It sounded reckless at the time, maybe even destructive.

But simplicity saved the company. And within a year, Apple was profitable again.

A decade later, it was the most valuable company on the

planet. Not because it did more, but because it did fewer things with absolute conviction.

Wells Fargo made a similar choice in the 1980s, although it looked far less glamorous. Instead of chasing global markets like Citibank, their CEO distilled it to one idea. There was more money to be made in Modesto than in Tokyo. That was not a metaphor. It was a challenge to an industry obsessed with expansion. Wells Fargo doubled down on being a regional bank. And they outperformed competitors with far more reach and complexity.

When Jim Collins studied companies that went from good to great, he found the same pattern. Companies excelled when they identified the intersection of three truths: what they could be the best at, what drove their economic engine, and what they were deeply passionate about.

Where those three circles overlapped, that was the focus. Anything outside that space was noise.

It sounds clean on paper. It almost feels intuitive. But in practice, it is brutally difficult.

Why Success Quietly Destroys Focus

If you want to see where focus begins to fracture, you don't have to look at failure. You have to look at success. Success is intoxicating. It convinces leaders that their instincts are sharper than they actually are. It inflates risk tolerance. It makes new opportunities feel inevitable, even necessary.

Success whispers, "If you were good at one thing, imagine how good you'll be at five."

And for executives, the temptation is everywhere. You live in rooms filled with new ideas. Analysts show you growth curves. Your board pushes you to expand. Vendors pitch you the next frontier. Mergers appear to solve multiple problems at once.

Every spreadsheet suggests synergy. Every chart points up and to the right.

It's easy to forget that many companies died from indigestion, not starvation.

But the far more subtle killer of strategic focus is not expansion. It is alignment masquerading as focus.

When Alignment Becomes an Echo Chamber

At first, alignment feels like the holy grail. Everyone nods during strategy discussions. Everyone uses the same language. Everyone references the same priorities. At the offsite, the walls are covered in Post-its that all point toward the same North Star.

It feels disciplined. Unified. Visionary.

But alignment and focus are not the same.

Nokia was aligned. Every part of the organization rallied around making exceptional mobile hardware. Meanwhile, Apple and Google were building ecosystems, not devices. Nokia stayed aligned all the way to irrelevance.

General Motors was aligned, too. They believed in offering something for everyone. A car for every customer segment. Every price point. Every style. Technically, that was alignment. But it wasn't focus.

Toyota, on the other hand, built its identity around one idea. Make exceptionally reliable cars. That's it. They didn't chase every segment. They didn't fragment their attention. They focused so tightly that the rest of the industry had to adapt to them.

The research calls it "performative focus." It's the illusion of focus created by consistent messaging rather than consistent choices. Everyone says the right things, but no one questions whether the strategy holds up under pressure.

Here are the signs you're in this zone:

A team that repeats the same strategy language without challenging it.

Data that contradicts the plan gets softened or buried.

Decisions get justified with slogans rather than analysis.

New ideas are dismissed with "that's not our focus," without real evaluation.

When you're inside this environment, it doesn't feel dishonest. It feels aligned. That's what makes it so dangerous. Groupthink wears the costume of clarity.

Jason sat in meetings like this and felt relief, not concern. Everyone sounded smart. Everyone agreed. The language was crisp. The decks were clean. It took him longer than he realized that nothing meaningful was being questioned.

Tools Alone Cannot Save You

There are tools that should protect focus. OKRs to define what matters, portfolio reviews, kill criteria, red teams, pre-mortems. These are proven mechanisms that force attention, discipline, and reduction.

They work well in healthy cultures.

They do almost nothing in unhealthy ones.

You can have perfect goals, numbers and a scorecard to measure what everything should look like on paper, but if your culture discourages dissent, those OKRs will anchor you to the wrong goals. You can run monthly portfolio reviews, but if the culture rewards "yes" and penalizes "no," every project will survive even when the data says it shouldn't.

You can assign devil's advocates, but if psychological safety is low, they will challenge politely rather than truthfully.

The tools themselves are not the weak link. Culture is.

When culture rewards agreement instead of honesty, people

stop telling the truth, and what looks like focus becomes an act instead of a practice.

The Diagnostic Chart below will reveal what sits underneath this illusion of focus: the emotional habits, the cultural signals, the unquestioned assumptions, and the dynamics that quietly distort how teams make decisions.

When you can see the system clearly, the theater dissolves, and real focus becomes possible.

Blind Spot 3: The Focus Fallacy

Element	Description	What It Looks Like in Leadership
Psychology Underneath	Desire for clarity and control leads to overvaluing alignment signals.	Leaders mistake everyone nodding for actual strategic focus.
Internal Pattern that Keeps It Alive	Groupthink, risk aversion, consensus chasing, false certainty.	Teams repeat the strategy language but don't execute true trade-offs.
Why Leaders Can't Self-Correct	Alignment feels good. Focus feels restrictive. Hard choices feel risky.	Leaders cling to unity instead of honesty.
Underlying Dynamics	Cognitive narrowing, cultural conformity, flawed feedback loops.	Companies drift, overextend, or chase too many priorities.

Blind Spot #4:
PERFORMANCE-BASED WORTH - WORTH TIED TO ACHIEVEMENT & STATUS

A specific pattern emerges quietly in high achievers. You can't spot it in their résumés or their board presentations. You see it in the way they talk to themselves after a failure. You see it in how quickly their mood shifts when they land a win. And if you listen closely, you hear it in the way they describe their ambition; a little too tightly, a little too urgently, as if their worth depends on keeping the momentum going.

For many executives, it does.

This blind spot is what psychologists call **performance-based self-worth.** It's the belief that your value as a person rises and falls based on how well you perform. It is a powerful motivator. It is also one of the most corrosive forces in executive life.

Not everyone with ambition falls into this trap. Protective factors exist. Social support. Healthy coping skills. Stable relationships. Humor. A life outside work. These things buffer the impact.

But as a general trend, the more someone ties their identity to achievement, the more vulnerable they become to emotional volatility and, eventually, burnout. And unlike some blind spots that appear only under extreme pressure, this one often starts early and grows with success.

What the Science Has Known for More Than a Century

The idea is not new. William James captured it in 1890 when he described self-esteem as the ratio of success to aspirations. Think about that for a moment. The higher your goals, the more your sense of worth depends on meeting them. It seems like simple math, but the emotional implications are brutal.

Modern research expanded on James's insight and turned it into measurable data. Jennifer Crocker at the University of Michigan spent years studying what she called **contingencies of self-worth**. She identified several domains where people stake their value: competition, academic success, approval, appearance, virtue, love, and work.

But not all domains are equal.

The ones tied to external performance are the ones that become unstable. Competition. Achievement. Others' approval. These are the domains most associated with anxiety, depression, defensiveness, and perfectionism.

When your value depends on performance, the stakes rise with every task. Every presentation. Every quarter. Every goal.

A win becomes proof you matter. A loss becomes proof you don't.

The Corporate Amplifier

The corporate environment magnifies this dynamic in a way James could never have anticipated. Organizations reward performance. They celebrate results. They promote based on outcomes. None of that is inherently harmful until the person internalizes it as identity.

A 2020 study on work-contingent self-esteem found something revealing. In the short term, tying your worth to work success looks productive. It fuels motivation. It produces effort. It drives results.

But over time, the cost emerges.

Higher burnout.

Higher exhaustion.

Higher work/family conflict.

Lower overall well-being.

Executives who rely on achievement to feel like "enough" begin sacrificing everything else to sustain that feeling. Rest becomes a threat. Boundaries feel irresponsible. And the cruel irony is that the more they sacrifice, the more depleted they become, undermining the performance they're trying to protect.

It becomes a feedback loop.

Run harder. Feel worse. Achieve less. Panic. Run harder.

The Roller Coaster No One Talks About

One of the clearest findings in the research is that performance-based self-worth creates emotional whiplash.

Good quarter? You feel energized, confident, alive.

Missed target? You feel exposed, ashamed, diminished.

And the swing doesn't stay constant. Studies show that over time, the highs get flatter, and the lows get deeper. The emotional system begins wearing down. Executives who once bounced back quickly now feel shaken by minor setbacks. Their emotional resilience erodes in silence.

Jason noticed the pattern before he named it for himself. Wins still brought relief, but not joy. Losses lingered longer than they should have. He started needing performance just to feel steady, not successful.

The burnout connection isn't speculative. It's direct.

A study of medical students, a population that mirrors executive psychology in many ways, found that those with high performance-based worth were significantly more likely to experience both exhaustion and disengagement. They weren't just tired. They were withdrawing from the very work that defined them.

That same pattern shows up across industries. High performers who define themselves by achievement end up least capable of recovering when something goes wrong.

The Hidden Organizational Costs

The personal costs are clear. What's less obvious is the damage this blind spot inflicts on the organization itself.

Innovation declines. People stop taking risks because failure feels too dangerous. They choose what guarantees success over what could create value.

Honesty erodes. When your worth depends on performance, you can't admit mistakes. You can't expose gaps. You can't ask for help.

Problems hide instead of surfacing. Teams become impression management engines instead of learning systems.

Resilience weakens and small setbacks feel existential. At the same time, external fluctuations, such as weather, consumer confidence, market cycles, create disproportionate emotional crashes.

Then a fixed mindset takes root. People strive to appear competent rather than become more competent. Growth stalls because growth requires being willing to look inexperienced.

None of this is intentional. It's psychological gravity.

The Collapse of Psychological Safety

And then there is the cultural impact.

Executives whose self-worth depends on performance create

cultures where truth becomes dangerous. If the leader cannot fail, neither can anyone else. If the leader cannot admit uncertainty, no one will speak up. If the leader needs constant validation, dissent becomes a threat.

Research in healthcare shows this vividly. In environments where mistakes are punished or hidden, error reporting plummets. Near misses go underground. Problems accumulate until they explode.

But in cultures that treat honest mistakes as opportunities for learning, error reporting increases dramatically while actual errors decline. Psychological safety saves lives.

In corporate settings, it saves companies.

Short-Term Thinking Takes Over

When your worth rises and falls with performance, long-term strategy becomes difficult. You are more vulnerable to short-termism, corner-cutting, and decisions driven by ego preservation rather than organizational health.

The Wells Fargo scandal, exposed in the fall of 2016, is a dramatic example of what happens when unrealistic performance demands combine with leaders whose identities are tied to results. Employees created millions of fraudulent accounts to avoid the shame of missing targets. The company paid billions in penalties. But the deeper wound was cultural, revealing a system that tied worth to performance so tightly that ethics had no room to breathe.

The research is blunt about this. When self-worth is on the line, people will take risks they'd never consider under healthy circumstances. They will hide the truth. They will bend rules. They will erode trust. And they will believe they are doing the right thing, because the alternative feels like personal failure.

The Human Cost

The most painful part of performance-based worth is not what it does to output. It's what it does to a person. Relationships suffer. Emotional vulnerability feels dangerous. Feedback triggers defensiveness. Collaboration becomes competition.

High performers who thrived in teams begin isolating themselves. Confidence becomes brittle.

Ambition becomes anxiety. Standards become self-punishment.

And the person who once felt energized by challenge now feels trapped by it.

This is why performance-based worth is such a powerful blind spot. It looks like drive. It looks like passion. It looks like commitment. But underneath, it is something far more fragile.

And unless you name it, you cannot change it.

The Diagnostic Chart below will map the deeper mechanics of this blind spot: the pressure that becomes identity, the stories that become rules, and the emotional patterns that turn ambition into anxiety.

Understanding the structure allows you to separate who you are from what you produce, and that separation changes everything.

Blind Spot 4: Performance-Based Worth

Element	Description	What It Looks Like in Leadership
Psychology Underneath	Self-worth tied to outcomes rather than identity.	Leaders feel euphoric after wins and ashamed after misses.
Internal Pattern that Keeps It Alive	Overwork, comparison, approval-seeking, perfectionistic self-critique.	Leaders sacrifice rest and relationships to protect their worth.
Why Leaders Can't Self-Correct	Success temporarily soothes the fear, reinforcing the cycle.	Leaders believe slowing down threatens their identity.
Underlying Dynamics	Reward circuitry, early attachment patterns, achievement conditioning.	Burnout, brittle confidence, inability to detach from work.

Blind Spot #5:

THE JUDGMENT TRAP - EMOTIONAL REACTIVITY VS. DISCERNMENT

There is a moment, often so quick you barely notice it, when your brain decides how you will respond to a situation. It happens long before you have time to think. A look from a board member. A curt email. A hesitation in someone's voice. Something lands wrong, and your body reacts before your mind catches up.

Neuroscience has mapped this with remarkable clarity. The amygdala, the part of your brain wired for threat detection, fires almost instantly. It was designed for survival in a very different world. One where hesitation meant danger. Physical danger. Life-ending danger. So, the amygdala learned to react first, question later.

In a leadership context, this ancient response becomes problematic.

While your amygdala is sounding an alarm, your prefrontal cortex, the part of your brain responsible for nuanced thinking, analysis, and judgment, momentarily goes offline.

Author Daniel Goleman called this an amygdala hijack, and the description feels accurate. Something in you has taken the wheel, and your better judgment hasn't been invited along for the ride.

During those moments, your field of vision, along with your emotional, cognitive, and relational abilities, narrows dramatically. You might fire off a sharp email. You might shut down completely. You might interpret neutral behavior as hostility. You might jump to conclusions that feel certain but are entirely driven by emotion, not discernment.

This is the dramatic version of the judgment trap, the one you tend to recognize afterward. The snapped comment. The meeting you wish you'd handled differently. The reaction that felt justified in the moment but regrettable in hindsight.

But the more dangerous version is quieter. It doesn't look like an outburst. It looks like certainty. Beliefs or a point of view you would go to the mat for. Like these examples:

A belief about someone's competence that calcifies over time.

A story you tell yourself about a colleague's motives.

A conclusion about a team's capability that you never revisit.

A suspicion that becomes fact simply because you've rehearsed it mentally long enough.

This slow, chronic version of judgment is harder to detect because it doesn't feel like reactivity. It feels like truth. You think you have evaluated the situation rationally. You think your perspective is accurate. But what you're really seeing is your own emotional residue, hardened into an assumption.

Jason didn't think of himself as reactive or assumptive. He thought of himself as observant. By the time he noticed how often his conclusions preceded his curiosity, they already felt like facts. He thought his decision-making was a rational superpower.

Buddhist psychology has studied this dynamic for centuries and offers a useful distinction.

It's a distinction between the judging mind and the discerning mind. The judging mind reacts with aversion. It labels. It condemns. It clings to narratives long after the moment has passed.

The discerning mind, by contrast, sees without attachment. It evaluates cleanly. It gathers information without personalizing it. It can say, "This isn't working," without slipping into, "They are the problem."

The difference is profound.

Judgment collapses complexity. It reduces people to caricatures. It assumes intention without inquiry.

Discernment, on the other hand, opens space. It invites curiosity. It asks what else might be true. It recognizes that behavior is often a symptom, not the root.

Another helpful lens comes from the Positive Intelligence (PQ) framework, which identifies the Judge as the brain's master saboteur. It is the voice that fault-finds in everything, in others, in circumstances, and relentlessly in yourself. It exaggerates danger. It magnifies flaws. It whispers that vigilance is safety, that criticism is intelligence, that cynicism is clarity.

But it is none of those things.

It is emotional reactivity dressed up as leadership.

The Judge doesn't just appear in heated moments. It operates constantly, coloring your interactions, tilting your perspective, and shaping your reactions before you realize you're reacting. It convinces you that its assessments are accurate reflections of reality rather than snapshots of your emotional state.

And because it also turns inward, the Judge reinforces your self-criticism too. It tells you that you should have known better. That you should always be composed. That any misstep confirms something defective about you. This is where leaders get stuck; in the exhausting loop of judging others and then judging themselves for judging others.

The research is unequivocal on the impact. When executives operate from emotional reactivity, their decision quality declines. Their ability to see nuance deteriorates. They miss critical information. They misread intent. They create atmospheres where people withhold truth because the emotional cost of honesty feels too high.

Cultures shaped by judgment tend to be fast-moving on the surface but brittle underneath. They run on pressure instead of clarity. Fear instead of curiosity. Correction instead of learning. In these environments, leaders are constantly reacting to symptoms instead of addressing causes, and organizations burn immense energy managing emotional fallout rather than making strategic progress.

But when leaders learn to interrupt this pattern, to slow the mental storm long enough for their prefrontal cortex to reengage, something shifts. Discernment returns. Options reappear. Conversations broaden. Leaders begin to see the person instead of the projection, the system instead of the story, the possibility instead of the threat.

The difference between judgment and discernment is not intelligence. It is not experience. It is not personality.

It is the state of mind you're using in the moment.

And most leaders do not realize how often they are making decisions from the wrong mind.

The Diagnostic Chart below reveals the architecture of the judgment reflex: the currents that pull you toward certainty, the stories that harden into conclusions, the emotions that masquerade as insight, and the dynamics that shape which "mind" you're using in any given moment.

When you can see the pattern with this level of clarity, the mind you choose to lead from becomes a conscious choice rather than an automatic reaction.

Blind Spot 5: The Judgment Trap

Element	Description	What It Looks Like in Leadership
Psychology Underneath	Amygdala-driven threat response creates fast, rigid judgments.	Leaders assume intent without evidence and misread neutral cues.
Internal Pattern that Keeps It Alive	Story-making, certainty inflation, negative attribution.	Leaders see people through old narratives, not current reality.
Why Leaders Can't Self-Correct	Judgment feels like discernment. Reactivity feels like truth.	Leaders double down instead of questioning first impressions.
Underlying Dynamics	Amygdala hijack, diminished prefrontal cortex activity, cognitive narrowing.	Damaged relationships, disengaged teams, repeated misinterpretations.

Blind Spot #6:

PERFECTIONISM'S PRISON - IMPOSSIBLE STANDARDS

There is a type of high achiever you might recognize who doesn't slow down, even when every signal in their life says they should. They keep refining. They keep polishing. They keep pushing themselves and everyone around them toward a standard that seems noble on the surface but becomes suffocating the closer you get to it.

That pattern has a name. Perfectionism.

And while the word often gets tossed around casually, the research behind it paints a far more serious picture.

Over the past three decades, perfectionism has increased by more than thirty percent across society. That means more people are setting standards they cannot realistically meet. More people are attaching their worth to flawless execution. And more people are burning out because the pressure is relentless and the target is constantly moving.

The toll is not just emotional. It is physiological.

Researchers at the University of New South Wales found that perfectionists experience higher rates of anxiety, depression, irritability, insomnia, headaches, and cognitive fog. It is not "stress." It is a full-body shutdown caused by never feeling good enough.

Physicians offer one of the clearest illustrations of this trend.

Roughly thirty percent are burned out at any given moment. Over the course of a career, that number rises to sixty percent. These are individuals trained to operate under pressure. Experts in resilience. And even they are collapsing under the weight of impossible standards.

What makes all of this even more disheartening is a finding that surprises almost everyone.

Perfectionists do not perform better.

A massive analysis of ninety-five studies found no evidence that perfectionism improves performance or output quality. None. High standards, yes. Perseverance, yes. But the obsessive, fear-driven pursuit of perfect outcomes? It does not translate into better results.

Cognitive science explains why. Once you consistently work more than fifty to fifty-five hours per week, your mental performance begins to decline. And the decline is steep. In fact, managers struggle to distinguish the work of someone pushing eighty hours from someone working fifty-five. The extra effort is invisible because the brain is already overextended.

In other words, perfectionists sacrifice their mental health for performance gains that do not exist.

Two Kinds of Perfectionism: One Helpful, One Harmful

Researchers now make an important distinction between two types of perfectionism. Understanding the difference matters, because one kind fuels growth while the other destroys it.

Perfectionistic strivings represent the healthier version. This is the part of you that cares deeply about craft, quality, and mastery. You set high standards because excellence inspires you.

You push yourself because improvement energizes you. Think of elite athletes or musicians who train intensely, knowing the work makes them better.

Perfectionistic concerns are the dangerous version. This is the fear-driven side. The part that believes mistakes define you. The part that expects judgment from others. The part that equates anything less than flawless with failure. It is not about vision. It is about fear. It is not about mastery. It is about self-protection.

The difference between the two is motivation.

Strivings pull you forward. Concerns chase you from behind.

Perfectionistic concerns are strongly correlated with all three components of burnout; exhaustion, cynicism, and a sense of inadequacy. When you fear failure, you overcommit. You avoid delegating. You spend hours correcting tiny imperfections that do not matter. You rewrite, rework, and redo. You wear yourself down in the name of protecting an image.

Jason told himself he was just being thorough. Letting something go unfinished felt irresponsible. Letting someone else handle it felt risky. By the time he noticed how much energy he was spending to prevent mistakes that rarely mattered, slowing down no longer felt like an option.

And when every task becomes high stakes, your nervous system never gets to rest.

The Organizational Cost of Perfection

Inside companies, perfectionism becomes more than a personal challenge. It becomes a cultural toxin. Harvard Business Review identifies three predictable ways perfectionism hurts business performance.

The first is prioritization failure. When everything feels important, nothing truly is. The perfectionist brain cannot distinguish the strategic from the trivial. A vendor email. A board packet. A customer proposal. A formatting preference. They all carry the same emotional weight. So, you either become paralyzed or overwhelmed trying to deliver on all of it.

Second, perfectionists feel morally obligated to overdeliver everywhere. Not just where it counts. Everywhere. That sense of moral duty traps them in a cycle where even minor tasks demand major energy.

Third, perfectionism clings to old habits long after they have stopped being effective. Changing a habit means risking a misstep. And for the perfectionist mind, any misstep feels intolerably dangerous. So outdated approaches stick around far beyond their useful life.

Some leaders point to icons like Steve Jobs or Stanley Kubrick as proof that perfectionism can coexist with genius. It is true that both demanded excellence. It is also true that both created environments where fear suppressed creativity and where some of the best ideas never made it to the table because people were afraid to bring anything less than perfect to them.

Perfectionistic leadership narrows the space for risk-taking. It stifles innovation. It encourages people to hide work until it is "perfect," which slows execution and reduces learning. And it fosters a culture where people stay quiet instead of offering imperfect but valuable ideas.

The Psychological Safety Problem

Teams led by perfectionists report significantly lower psychological safety. That is not surprising. When the leader cannot tolerate mistakes, neither can anyone else. When the leader has impossible standards for themselves, those standards spread through the company without ever being spoken.

Research in healthcare underscores this dynamic with

painful clarity. In environments where mistakes are punished or hidden, error reporting collapses. Staff members conceal near-misses. Problems multiply quietly. Risks compound until they erupt.

But when organizations shift to a learning culture, one that treats honest mistakes as data, error reporting increases dramatically. Actual errors decrease. People share earlier, collaborate more, and innovate more freely. The difference comes down to one thing: whether imperfection is allowed to exist.

Perfectionism kills psychological safety at its root.

Short-Term Thinking, Long-Term Damage

When a leader's self-worth is tied to being flawless, short-term thinking begins to dominate decision-making. The urgency behind "getting this right" overwhelms the need to get the strategy right. Leaders chase quick wins to avoid discomfort. They avoid experiments that might expose gaps. They ask teams to hit aggressive targets even when those targets are unrealistic.

The Wells Fargo account scandal became a case study in how perfectionistic pressure can distort culture. When leaders set targets that were nearly impossible and tied those targets to identity and survival, employees made choices that violated ethics. Not because they were unethical, but because the emotional threat of missing the goal was too high.

Perfectionism, when scaled, becomes systemic dysfunction.

The Human Impact

The most painful cost of perfectionism is not organizational. It is personal.

People driven by impossible standards often feel alone in their struggle. They believe they are the only ones who cannot meet their own expectations. They judge themselves harshly and assume others are judging just as harshly. Relationships suffer because perfectionism leaves little room for vulnerability. And over time, the very traits that once fueled their success begin to undermine it.

Perfectionists are often admired early in their careers as disciplined, detail-oriented, and reliable. But the standard keeps rising. The pressure compounds. What once looked like strength becomes a burden they cannot set down.

If excellence is the pursuit of something meaningful, perfectionism is the fear of being exposed.

And until you see the difference, the prison stays invisible.

The Diagnostic Chart below will help you see the deeper structure of this blind spot: the fear that masquerades as excellence, the internal pressure that disguises itself as standards, the emotional reflexes that turn responsibility into self-punishment, and the reinforcing loops that make flawless execution feel like the only safe option.

When you understand the forces beneath the surface, you can finally separate genuine excellence from the quiet, consuming fear that keeps raising the bar until you disappear beneath it.

Blind Spot 6: Perfectionism's Prison

Element	Description	What It Looks Like in Leadership
Psychology Underneath	Fear of failure and fear of judgment masked as "high standards."	Leaders redo work, overcorrect, or avoid delegation.
Internal Pattern that Keeps It Alive	Catastrophic thinking, unrealistic benchmarks, hypervigilance.	Everything becomes mission-critical, even trivial tasks.
Why Leaders Can't Self-Correct	Perfectionism feels like responsibility. Imperfection feels dangerous.	Leaders defend impossible expectations as "the right way."
Underlying Dynamics	Stress hormone overactivation, cognitive overload, habit loops of fear.	Exhaustion, stalled innovation, fragile confidence.

Blind Spot #7:

THE ISOLATION TRAP – ATLAS SYNDROME

Loneliness comes in a special flavor for leaders and is rarely talked about. It's not the surface kind where you eat lunch alone or wish you had more friends. This is a deeper, more private separation from the people around you. A kind that grows slowly, almost invisibly, as the responsibilities of leadership accumulate.

Half of CEOs report feeling lonely in their roles. More than sixty percent believe that loneliness hurts their performance. These numbers rise every year, and not because CEOs suddenly became less social. Something else is happening under the surface.

Tim Cook once said that being CEO of Apple is "sort of a lonely job." He meant it. And he's not even an outlier.

In 2024, over half of CEOs reported serious mental health challenges, including anxiety, depression, and symptoms of burnout. That's a dramatic increase from the year before. Something in the structure of modern leadership is creating conditions that are quietly draining people.

But here's the important distinction. It isn't *loneliness* that hurts executives most. It's *isolation.*

Loneliness is the feeling of being alone. Isolation is the belief that you cannot share the truth of your experience with anyone. Most CEOs are surrounded by people constantly. They are in meetings, on calls, traveling with teams, giving presentations. Their calendars are overflowing.

And yet many feel unable to share the burdens they carry.

They put on the armor. They hold the line. They tighten their grip so nothing slips.

This is the Atlas Syndrome.

In Greek mythology, Atlas is the Titan condemned to carry the sky on his shoulders. Not for a day. Not for a season. For eternity. He doesn't ask for help because help is not an option. He doesn't rest because rest is impossible. His burden becomes his identity.

Executives fall into this mindset for different reasons. Some fear that showing weakness will undermine their authority. Some worry about burdening their teams. Some convince themselves that no one else will understand. And some simply don't want to admit, even to themselves, that the weight is too heavy.

The research on this is stark. Isolation erodes confidence. It diminishes self-efficacy. It distorts judgment. And it increases the likelihood of burnout. Social isolation is associated with a thirty-two percent higher risk of all-cause mortality. Loneliness increases that risk by fourteen percent.

These are not abstract numbers. They reflect real psychological and physiological consequences.

The emotional path into isolation often begins subtly. You stop sharing small concerns because you don't want to appear unsteady. You stop raising bigger concerns because the stakes feel too high. You stop asking for help because asking makes you feel exposed. Before long, your world narrows. You are carrying things alone that were never meant to be carried alone.

Jason couldn't remember the last time he'd said, *This is heavier than I expected*, out loud.

Not because there was no one around, but because he no longer knew who it would be safe to say it to.

The load increases. The sense of capability decreases.

Researchers describe Atlas Syndrome as the widening gap between the weight of the challenge and your belief in your ability to respond. The challenge grows faster than your perceived strength. Each day demands more. Each week adds pressure. And slowly, the burden becomes internalized as something you *should* be able to hold, even when you can't.

This creates a predictable spiral.

Isolation fuels burnout. Burnout increases emotional volatility. Emotional volatility leads to withdrawal. Withdrawal deepens isolation. And the cycle repeats.

One of the most surprising findings comes from a Stanford study showing that two-thirds of CEOs do not receive any external coaching or structured leadership advice. Two-thirds of the people in the most demanding leadership roles in the world have no formal support. No outside perspective. No lifeline.

We talk about resilience, performance, decision quality. We talk about innovation and accountability. But we rarely talk about support structures. And without support, even the strongest leaders begin to fracture.

Inside the brain, the early signs are subtle. Emotional swings that appear without clear triggers. Alternating hope and despair. Bursts of focus followed by collapse. Irritability that feels disproportionate. A growing sense of indifference. A slow slide into numbness.

These are not personality flaws. They're the neurological consequences of carrying too much, too privately, for too long.

What makes this blind spot so insidious is that it masquerades as strength. You tell yourself you're protecting your team. You tell yourself you're shielding your board. You tell yourself it's better if you carry the pressure alone. But what you're really doing is stepping deeper into the Atlas role without noticing how much heavier the sky is getting.

Isolation is not the absence of people. It is the absence of shared truth.

And when leaders cannot share truth, even with advisors, peers, teams, or especially themselves, the consequences are predictable and painful.

This is the core of Blind Spot #7.

Not solitude. Not independence. Not privacy, but isolation. The quiet, private, heavy belief that you must carry it alone.

The Diagnostic Chart below will help you see the full architecture of this pattern: the identity wiring that pulls you toward over-responsibility, the emotional habits that confuse isolation with strength, the internal narratives that make support feel dangerous, and the reinforcing loops that slowly convince you that carrying everything alone is the only way to lead.

When the underlying system becomes visible, the weight begins to shift, and the possibility of sharing the load stops feeling like a threat and starts feeling like relief.

Blind Spot 7: The Isolation Trap

Element	Description	What It Looks Like in Leadership
Psychology Underneath	Identity fused with responsibility. Support feels like weakness.	Leaders hide stress, over function, and avoid vulnerability.
Internal Pattern that Keeps It Alive	Over-responsibility, emotional withdrawal, distrust of others' competence.	Leaders stop asking for help and start doing everything themselves.
Why Leaders Can't Self-Correct	The burden reinforces identity; being needed feels like worth.	Leaders believe their suffering is necessary for success.
Underlying Dynamics	Stress isolation loops, diminished oxytocin response, distorted self-efficacy.	Leadership loneliness, emotional collapse, or sudden burnout.

Blind Spot #8:

TRANSACTIONAL RELATIONSHIPS - THE EROSION OF AUTHENTIC CONNECTION

A subtle shift happens as leaders rise inside an organization. At first, work relationships feel natural. They begin the way most human connections do; with curiosity, humor, shared pressure, late-night problem-solving, the small rituals that turn colleagues into companions.

But over time, something changes. The language becomes more formal. The expectations become more rigid. And the relationships become increasingly defined by utility. You start noticing who can help you, who slows you down, who solves problems, who creates them, who has influence, and who drains your energy.

This is not intentional. It is not malicious. It is simply the culture most of us are raised in. A system where value is assigned based on what a person produces rather than who they are.

The modern workplace has perfected this reduction. Performance reviews that rank people. KPIs that convert effort into metrics. Organizational charts that literally draw boxes around human beings. None of these systems are inherently harmful. They are necessary for coordination and accountability. But they create a mental framework that is easy to internalize: the people around me are resources. They exist to help things function.

Once that framework takes hold, something dangerous begins to happen.

A 2019 study from the Journal of Business Ethics found that senior executives reported sixty-eight percent fewer genuine friendships at work than employees just starting their careers. The higher someone climbed, the more their relationships were described in terms of strategic value, access, influence, and functional alignment, not trust, not warmth, not shared humanity.

This pattern is not isolated to corporate life. It is cultural. Even the way we talk about connection has shifted. "Networking" used to be a byproduct of relationships. Now it's an action item. We build networks. We expand them. We optimize them. LinkedIn is both the symptom and the accelerant, a platform that turns human connection into a professional currency.

The language of human resources reinforces the message. People are resources. Assets. Headcount. Capacity. We talk about deploying them, acquiring them, reallocating them. Slowly, quietly, we absorb the message: a person's worth lies in their function.

Neuroscience reveals how deeply this affects the brain.

When leaders engage in transactional thinking, fMRI scans show increased activation in regions associated with analytical processing. These are the same systems used for logic puzzles and problem-solving.

The same scans show that reduced activation in areas tied to empathy, emotional resonance, and social bonding happen with analytical processing. The brain literally shifts into a mode where people are seen as instruments to achieve outcomes rather than beings to connect with.

This is not a character flaw. It is conditioning.

Dr. Amy Cuddy's research at Harvard gives us another lens. Humans evaluate others along two dimensions: warmth and competence. Warmth predicts trust. Competence predicts respect. In transactional relationships, leaders hyperfocus on competence. What can this person do for me? How do they help me achieve my goals? Warmth, the predictor of trust and psychological safety, fades from attention.

The result is what researchers call **instrumental relationships**, meaning connections that exist for function, not for meaning. These relationships look efficient. They feel efficient. They even produce short-term results. But they carry a profound emotional and organizational cost.

Studies of transactional cultures show predictable outcomes:

People leave more often.

Stress hormones stay elevated longer.

Creativity declines because risk-taking feels unsafe.

Anxiety and depression increase.

Commitment erodes because loyalty becomes conditional.

When you treat people as utilities, they reciprocate in kind. They protect themselves. They give only what is necessary. They avoid vulnerability. They do not invest emotionally because they correctly sense that emotional investment is not valued.

This creates what game theorists call a **defection equilibrium**. Everyone acts in their own interest because they assume everyone else will do the same. Collaboration becomes cautious. Honesty becomes filtered. Trust becomes fragile.

The consequences reach far beyond culture. They shape behavior.

Leaders begin filtering interactions through usefulness.

"Is this person helpful to me?"

"Does this connection advance anything?"

"Is this meeting worth my time?"

The utility filter becomes automatic. You stop interacting with people who cannot help you. And if you do see them, you see only their function.

Jason caught himself scanning conversations for usefulness before listening for meaning.

He still smiled. Still asked polite questions. But somewhere along the way, connection started feeling like a distraction instead of the point.

The Transactional Leader

Another subtle mechanism emerges: the reciprocity ledger. Every interaction becomes a transaction. Every favor is logged. Every gesture is weighed. Everything becomes about fairness and balance. Virtually nothing feels unconditional.

Then comes the disposability mindset. If someone is only as valuable as their utility, they become interchangeable the moment someone more useful appears. People sense this. They may not articulate it, but they feel it in the way leaders look at them, speak to them, prioritize them.

And when leaders shut down empathy to sustain this mode of operating, something else shuts down too. The emotional circuitry that helps us understand fatigue in someone's voice, discouragement in their posture, hope in their ideas, or fear in their silence. Those cues blur. Eventually, they disappear.

The final mechanism is cultural spread. Transactional thinking is contagious. People mimic the relational norms of those above them. If the leader treats people as functions, the organization learns to do the same. Lunches become networking opportunities. Introductions become utility statements. Even friendships get evaluated for strategic worth.

This is why transactional thinking becomes a blind spot.

To the leader, it does not feel wrong. It feels efficient, smart, and strong.

But efficiency without humanity creates brittle systems. Smart decisions without empathy become costly ones. And leadership without relationship becomes manipulation in nicer clothing.

Here is the paradox the research makes clear: when you strip humanity out of relationships, performance declines. Turnover rises. Trust disappears. Psychological safety collapses. Innovation stalls. People retreat into self-protection. Teams do the minimum required to survive. No one brings their full effort because no one feels fully seen.

The core of Blind Spot #8.

Google's Project Aristotle, a massive research effort into what makes teams effective, landed on a stunning conclusion. The single strongest predictor of team performance was not talent, not experience, not credentials, not skill.

It was psychological safety. The feeling that you matter as a person, your voice is welcome, and that you will not be punished for showing up imperfectly.

Transactional relationships kill psychological safety at its foundation.

The antidote is not to abandon structure or performance expectations. It is to remember that performance is carried by people, and people flourish through connection. The best work comes from humans who feel valued, not extracted.

From relationships built on trust, not exchange.

When you reduce someone to their utility, you limit the depth of what you can create together.

When you honor their humanity, the possibilities multiply.

At the end of our careers, the metrics fade. The deals blur. The wins soften. What remains and what people carry with them is whether we saw them, not just used them. Whether we treated them as human.

The worst thing about this Blind Spot is not that we rely on people. But that we forget they are people.

The Diagnostic Chart below will help you see the deeper

workings of this pattern: the subtle shifts that turn people into functions, the emotional habits that dull empathy, the cultural cues that reward efficiency over connection, and the internal narratives that make utility feel safer than humanity.

Once the structure is visible, the distance becomes easier to understand, and the path back to genuine connection becomes far clearer than it ever felt from inside the pattern.

Blind Spot 8: Transactional Relationships

Element	Description	What It Looks Like in Leadership
Psychology Underneath	Competence-over-warmth bias and analytical dominance.	Leaders evaluate people by output, not relationship.
Internal Pattern that Keeps It Alive	Utility filtering, scorekeeping, disposability mindset.	Leaders interact conditionally: "What can you do for me?"
Why Leaders Can't Self-Correct	Transactional behaviors feel efficient and logical.	Leaders miss declining trust as metrics still move.
Underlying Dynamics	Decreased empathy activation, heightened analytical circuitry.	Low psychological safety, high turnover, shallow collaboration.

Blind Spot #9:
BOUNDARY COLLAPSE - WORK CONSUMING ALL OF LIFE

Burnout doesn't always come from overwork or exhaustion or pressure, at least not directly. It comes from something far more subtle. Something that grows so gradually it becomes invisible until it completely overtakes you. It happens when the boundary between work and life dissolves so thoroughly that you can no longer tell where one ends and the other begins.

This is boundary collapse. And for modern leaders, it has become almost universal.

Harvard Business School conducted a study showing that executives spend seventy-two percent of their waking hours connected to work through email, messaging platforms, notifications, dashboards, and the constant drip of digital requests.

But the statistics miss the deeper truth. The brain carries work even during the remaining twenty-eight percent. That is the part no one measures. The part where you're physically present with the people you love while your mind is still in the meeting you just left.

The real danger is not the hours. It is the mental occupation.

Cognitive Load Persistence

Dr. Diane Hamilton, in her work on burnout, explains that constant change is exhausting not because change is inherently bad, but because it prevents the brain from reaching closure.

The mind needs cycles. Effort followed by completion. Challenge followed by resolution. When tasks never end, when goals reset immediately, when the pace outstrips the mind's ability to categorize an experience as "finished," something crucial fails to happen.

The brain never gets the signal that the challenge is over.

Researchers call this cognitive load persistence. The mind remains activated long after the work itself has stopped. Your prefrontal cortex, which handles decision-making and executive function, does not power down. It hums in the background, running warm, never fully recovering.

Imagine leaving a car engine running in the garage twenty-four hours a day. Nothing catastrophic happens at first. But the wear accumulates, quietly and relentlessly. The same thing happens to leaders who never mentally disengage from work. You may sleep. You may relax on the couch. You may go to dinner. But your cognitive engine never cools.

Over time, chronic activation rewires the brain.

Stress hormones stay elevated. Cortisol remains high and the body begins prioritizing survival over restoration. Sleep becomes shallow. Fatigue becomes your baseline. And your emotional resilience erodes without warning.

This is why people who appear highly driven suddenly feel apathetic. Confident executives suddenly lose their footing. Leaders who once loved their work start feeling trapped by it. Their systems are depleted long before they realize anything is wrong.

Boundary collapse looks like passion from the outside and it feels like commitment from the inside. But biologically, it functions like slow, continuous trauma.

When Boundaries Disappear

And here's the part many leaders don't want to admit: the collapse is often self-inflicted.

The leaders most at risk are the ones who love their work. They are energized by it. Inspired by it. Fed by it. They stay up late because they want to, not because someone asked them to. They check their phones because they're excited, not pressured. They use downtime to strategize. They use vacations to "think at a higher level." They use hobbies as extensions of performance.

This is what makes boundary collapse so dangerous. It masquerades as fulfillment.

When work feels like play, boundaries feel optional. When achievement feels like joy, limits feel restrictive. When your identity fuses with your role, stepping away feels like stepping out of yourself.

Researchers call this identity fusion. It's when what you do becomes who you are.

Someone asks how you're doing, and you answer with updates from work. Someone asks who you are, and you give your title. Your LinkedIn profile becomes more descriptive than your real life. Even conversations with strangers drift instantly toward professional topics because it feels like the only part of you that is interesting.

In Jason's case, he noticed how quickly every conversation bent back toward work.

Not because anyone pushed it there, but because he didn't know what else to say.

When he tried to picture himself outside his role, the image felt strangely blank.

And because the modern workplace rewards this, the collapse accelerates.

The Availability Cascade

There's a second mechanism researchers identified: the availability cascade. It begins innocently. One Sunday email. One late-night Slack message. One time you check your phone at dinner. Each small breach becomes a precedent. The expectation sets itself. Suddenly, responsiveness becomes a metric of loyalty. Your presence becomes synonymous with commitment. And your availability becomes proof of your value.

Then comes the optimization trap:

Everything is measured by productivity.

Running becomes a performance enhancer.

Family time becomes a scheduled block to "maximize quality."

Rest becomes a tactical recovery period to ensure better output.

Even leisure becomes transactional.

None of this looks alarming at first. It looks like discipline. It feels like focus and control.

But beneath it, something essential is being lost. It's the ability to be a human who works, instead of a worker who occasionally remembers they are human.

Researchers studying burnout in physicians witnessed the same erosion. In fields with high responsibility and constant urgency, work expands into every available space. People begin evaluating life choices through professional efficiency rather than personal fulfillment. And when life becomes something to optimize, joy becomes something accidental.

And here is the final, most painful part of boundary collapse:

once your identity fuses with work, every setback becomes personal.

A missed target becomes a wound. A failed project becomes humiliation. A critical email becomes existential.

When work becomes life, failure becomes identity. That is the heart of Blind Spot #9.

Not the long hours or the constant connectivity. It's the quiet belief that your life is expendable as long as your work is thriving.

By the time a leader recognizes the collapse, the system that should protect them is already gone. The boundaries that once separated roles, spaces, identities, and emotional states have dissolved. And rebuilding them requires a completely different kind of strength, not more endurance, but more self-awareness.

Boundary collapse is not a sign of dedication. It is a sign of depletion disguised as devotion. And naming it is the first step toward getting your life back.

The Diagnostic Chart below will help you see the deeper structure of this collapse: the identity patterns that blur your limits, the emotional habits that turn overextension into normalcy, the narratives that convince you your availability is the same as your value, and the internal forces that make it so difficult to protect the edges of your life.

When the system becomes visible, the pattern finally stops feeling like a personal failing and starts looking like what it truly is: an internal architecture that was never meant to hold this much weight without support.

Blind Spot 9: Boundary Collapse

Element	Description	What It Looks Like in Leadership
Psychology Underneath	Identity fusion with work and chronic cognitive activation.	Leaders think about work constantly, even when "off."
Internal Pattern that Keeps It Alive	Loss of self outside work.	Leaders don't honor family time.
Why Leaders Can't Self-Correct	Work feels rewarding; rest feels wasteful.	Leaders can't imagine stepping away. Work = identity.
Underlying Dynamics	Persistent cortisol elevation, lack of closure cycles.	Burnout masked as devotion, shrinking personal life.

Blind Spot #10:

THE COMPETENCE ILLUSION – CONFUSING KNOWLEDGE WITH PRACTICE

High performers fall into this particular trap more often than anyone else. It doesn't show up in performance reviews, and it doesn't look like a flaw. In fact, it feels like strength. You feel capable. You feel informed. You feel prepared. You think you understand yourself, your triggers, your habits, your stress cycles. You can even explain them to others with precision.

And that is exactly what makes the trap so dangerous.

The costliest blind spot in leadership is not ignorance. It is the belief that knowledge is the same as mastery. That understanding a concept is the same as embodying it. That being able to articulate a practice means you're actually practicing it.

Psychologists call this the knowing–doing gap. It is the quiet gulf between what we intellectually understand and what we consistently live. And it is one of the biggest predictors of burnout, relapse, emotional regression, and stalled recovery.

You see this everywhere. You see leaders who can define emotional intelligence while blowing up at their teams. Leaders who can describe the neuroscience of mindfulness while running on adrenaline and anxiety. Leaders who talk about boundaries while answering emails at midnight. Leaders who understand stress cycles while living in a perpetual one themselves.

They know better. They don't do better.

It's not hypocrisy. It's neuroscience.

A study out of Stanford makes this painfully clear. Participants were taught the full model of habit formation. They learned how cues trigger routines. They learned how reward cycles create neural pathways. They could explain the basal ganglia's role in repetition. Six weeks later, ninety-two percent failed to change a single habit.

They had the knowledge, but they lacked the integration.

Knowledge vs. Integration

This is the essence of the competence illusion. When you know something intellectually, the brain gets a hit of satisfaction. It feels like progress. It feels like clarity. It feels like control. But none of that knowledge transfers into behavior automatically.

The part of the brain that understands a concept is not the part of the brain that executes habits.

Your prefrontal cortex is the brilliant strategist. But habit lives in the basal ganglia, the autopilot system that runs the majority of your day without conscious thought. These two systems do not communicate efficiently. We end up believing something that feels true but is completely false.

"I understand it; therefore, I am doing it."

But understanding is not doing. It never has been. That disconnect becomes even more extreme in high achievers.

The more competent you are intellectually, the more likely you are to confuse comprehension with embodiment. You gather knowledge quickly. You absorb frameworks easily. You connect concepts effortlessly. And because you're good at it, you assume the rest will unfold naturally.

Except it doesn't.

The research shows that the more expertise someone has, the more susceptible they are to cognitive illusion. Confidence rises faster than competence. Knowledge becomes armor rather than access. Leaders collect certifications and books and trainings, not because they intend to practice them, but because the knowledge itself feels like progress.

But knowledge without practice creates a unique kind of suffering.

You can explain exactly why you are overwhelmed while still being overwhelmed.

You understand precisely why your stress patterns keep repeating while continuing to repeat them.

You can name every saboteur in your mind while being run by all of them.

This gap between knowing and doing slowly becomes torture. You see the problem clearly. You understand the solution. And still, nothing changes.

Jason could explain his patterns with unsettling accuracy. The stress cycle and overcommitment. The false urgency.

What he couldn't explain was why knowing all of that hadn't changed a thing.

It's like being a physical therapist with chronic back pain. A financial planner drowning in debt or

a physician ignoring their own symptoms.

It is not incompetence. It is disconnection. The problem is not failure. The problem is the belief that understanding protects you from failing.

Knowledge soothes the ego. Practice rewires the brain. And until you practice, nothing changes.

The Diagnostic Chart below will help you see the full internal structure of this illusion: the confidence that rises from understanding, the habits that remain untouched by

insight alone, the emotional patterns that pull you back into familiar behaviors, and the reinforcing loops that convince you that knowing should be enough.

When the system becomes visible, the disconnect between comprehension and practice finally makes sense, and the path toward true embodiment becomes far easier to see.

Blind Spot 10: The Competence Illusion

Element	Description	What It Looks Like in Leadership
Psychology Underneath	Cognitive illusion that understanding equals mastery.	Leaders explain skills they don't actively practice.
Internal Pattern that Keeps It Alive	Practice erosion, identity protection, intellectual overconfidence.	"I know this already" replaces doing the work.
Why Leaders Can't Self-Correct	Knowledge feels like progress; practice feels unnecessary.	Leaders plateau or regress despite high insight.
Underlying Dynamics	Prefrontal understanding vs. basal ganglia habits.	Leaders relapse under stress, despite knowing better.

Section 4:
The Reset

From Awareness to Integration: How Leaders Rebuild from the Inside Out

There is a quiet that comes after recognition of your Blind Spots. Not silence, that would be too overwhelming. But a softening. A loosening. A sense that the frantic motion inside you has finally stopped trying to outrun itself.

When you see your Blind Spots clearly, the shift doesn't begin with fireworks. It begins with exhaling. With the kind of understanding that settles deeper than thought. With the subtle knowing that you cannot return to the version of yourself who didn't yet see the blind spots.

And it isn't because you did anything wrong. It's because now you understand the cost of leading in the dark.

You've mapped the loops you've lived inside, sometimes for years.

You've seen the invisible architecture beneath your reactions.

You've felt the weight of storylines that were written long before your first leadership role yet shaped every decision you made inside it.

You've walked through the architecture of your patterns.

You've witnessed how old wiring shaped not only your leadership, but your capacity to breathe inside your own story.

You've seen the cost, in money, in metrics, but also in the quiet places: energy, trust, joy, presence, connection.

And with that recognition comes something unexpected.

Once you see those patterns as hard wiring, not as character flaws, not as personal failings or destiny, then something opens. Possibility enters, almost shyly at first. Not the kind that demands more of you.

Not the kind that pushes you toward the next finish line you never truly wanted.

A gentler possibility. A grounded possibility. The kind that waits for you rather than chases you.

Awareness is not an indictment. It's an invitation. Just like a reset isn't a collapse or a reinvention. It's a bold declaration that you're "starting over." It's not a productivity cleanse or a new system to force yourself through.

A reset is the slow, steady return to yourself. To the self beneath the armor, the self beneath the titles, and to the self who didn't need to prove worth, only express it.

This is where leadership begins to shift from strain to solidity. Where clarity replaces pressure.

Where emotional infrastructure is rebuilt not as scaffolding to hold you up, but as a foundation strong enough to move with you.

This is the place where boundaries become acts of honor, not guilt. Where worth untethers from output.

Where the original reason you stepped into leadership, the reason buried under deadlines, expectations, and the long shadow of perfectionism, rises back into view.

The blind spots you encountered in these pages were never indictments. They were illuminations.

Every leader you've ever admired has walked this same internal terrain. Every leader who rises eventually meets themselves in a way they can no longer avoid.

And every leader who sustains excellence learns this truth:

You cannot outpace your inner world. You can only learn to lead from within it.

And that learning doesn't come from force; not from more effort, more hours, more strategies, or more iron-willed promises whispered at midnight.

It comes from guided reset. From supported recalibration and from the patient, compassionate unwinding of beliefs that once protected you but no longer serves your becoming.

Your path does not lead toward more pressure. It leads toward alignment. Toward leadership that doesn't cost your identity or your wellbeing.

It leads toward a way of moving through the world that strengthens rather than depletes.

You have already completed the first and hardest step: You've seen what you could not see before.

From here, the inner work deepens, not through force, but through curiosity. Not through perfection, but through presence. Not through trying to become someone new, but through remembering who you are underneath the noise.

And you do not have to navigate that remembering alone.

Awareness begins the reset.

Support carries it forward.

Integration anchors it in your life.

But Blind Spots, by their nature, cannot be dismantled from the inside.

Now you understand that, too.

The doorway has opened. The frantic pace can finally be released. And a new architecture of leadership, calm, grounded, deeply human, waits for you, steady and patient, for when you choose to begin.

WHAT THE RESET PROCESS LOOKS LIKE

The work you've done in these pages was not intellectual. It was internal.

You've examined parts of yourself most leaders never pause long enough to see. You've recognized the patterns that once protected you but now hold you back. And you've begun the process of understanding why your leadership has felt heavier, faster, or more fragile than you expected.

If what you discovered in these chapters stirred something in you:

like a moment of recognition...

a sense of relief...

a quiet understanding that the way you've been operating is no longer sustainable...

you're not alone.

Every leader reaches this point. Not the point of breaking, but the point of *awakening*, where the internal world becomes too important to ignore and the old patterns stop being compatible with the life you want.

You could attempt to do this entirely on your own: analyze your patterns, rewrite your wiring, and challenge the beliefs constructed in the shadows.

But you don't have to navigate that transition alone.

This is the work I do every day with leaders and executives who have succeeded outwardly yet struggle inwardly with the strain of their own patterns.

Together, we rebuild the internal architecture that allows them to lead without collapsing into urgency, without overidentifying with performance, and without sacrificing the parts of themselves that once made leadership meaningful.

If you feel ready for that kind of guided reset; not a program, not a system, not a quick fix, but a real partnership in rebuilding the way you lead, I'm here.

No pressure.

No expectation.

Just an open door.

I hope this book has been helpful to you in your journey. Please take a moment to leave a review:

https://amzn.to/466rQmc

Work with Julien

If you'd like to explore whether this work is right for you, you can reach Julien directly here:

Contact Email: jgodbarge@gemconsultingsolutions.com

Website: www.TenBlindSpots.com

Private Consultation:

To schedule a confidential conversation about your leadership patterns, burnout risk, or next stage of professional growth, visit: **www.TenBlindSpots.com**

If something in this book resonated with the challenges you've been navigating alone, reach out when the time feels right.

You've already begun the reset, but you don't have to finish it without support.

Resources & Tools

SUPPORT MATERIALS TO DEEPEN YOUR AWARENESS AND CONTINUE YOUR RESET.

This book is designed to help you see what's been operating beneath the surface of your leadership, the patterns, pressures, and emotional habits that often go unnoticed until they create strain.

The resources in this section are here to support your continued reflection. They are not meant to replace the deeper, guided work of a reset, but to give you structured ways to explore what you've already begun to uncover.

Each tool is to be used slowly, thoughtfully, and without self-judgment. Move through them at your own pace. Return to them when something rises to the surface. Use them to track your insights, to clarify your patterns, and to prepare for the next stage of your development.

These resources are companions, not assignments.

Visit www.TenBlindSpots.com for additional resources and tools.

Acknowledgments

Every book is a collaboration, even when the writing itself takes place in quiet rooms and solitary mornings. This one is no different. It was written not only from personal experience and professional practice, but from years of conversations with leaders who trusted me with their fears, their doubts, their exhaustion, and their hopes. To those leaders, the ones who opened the door to their internal world and allowed me to walk with them through it, thank you. Your courage shaped these pages more than anything else.

I am deeply grateful to the colleagues and mentors who challenged my assumptions, expanded my thinking, and helped refine the frameworks that ultimately became the foundation of this book. Your influence lives in these insights, in the quiet spaces between each chapter, and in the work that unfolds long after the last page is turned.

In particular, I want to thank Boris Bajlovic, a longtime colleague and close friend whose conversations always bring depth and unexpected perspectives. Your unwavering support through the highs and lows has meant more than you know.

Kevin Long and Leonard Schulz, your grit, persistence, and optimistic attitude are a constant source of inspiration. Watching you build something remarkable through sheer determination reminds me what's possible when you refuse to quit.

Jason Woodward, a successful CEO whom I had the privilege to coach and guide. Your willingness to trust the process, lean into the work, and stay present through moments of discomfort speaks volumes about your leadership. Watching you translate insight into meaningful, lasting change has been one of the most rewarding confirmations of this work's impact.

Dan Casciano and Carter Cheskey, you've taught me more about the world of M&A and investment banking than I ever expected to learn. Those lessons shaped not just my career but how I think about business itself.

Brett Bacho, thank you for the opportunity to work with you. Your patience and kindness have taught me as much about leadership as any book ever could.

Denise Vivas, a dear friend and former colleague whose marketing instincts are as sharp as her perspective is generous. Thank you for being part of the beta reader program and for offering feedback that was both candid and deeply insightful. Your ability to see what resonates, and what doesn't, helped strengthen this book in ways that truly matter.

And Jim Shultz, your strategic vision and courage in leadership remain unmatched. Thank you for being my very first coaching client and for trusting me before I had fully learned to trust myself.

To my friends and family, thank you for the grounding, the patience, and the presence that made this work possible. You reminded me, again and again, that the best leadership begins at home and within the self. Your support was the private architecture behind every public idea.

To my parents, thank you for your unconditional love and support and for the foresight to insist that a boy growing up in rural France in the 1980s learn computers and English at a young age. You saw the world changing before most did, and you prepared me to thrive in it.

To my sister Anne, your support and expertise in corporate

coaching were instrumental to this work. Having a sibling who truly understands this world made all the difference.

To my brother Colin, thank you for always being willing to lend your sharp intellect to my projects. Your contributions sharpened my thinking in ways I couldn't have managed alone.

To my children, Matt, Chris, and Alex, you are my biggest fans and knowing that has carried me through more than you realize. Your belief in me means everything.

And to my wife Sharon, thank you for your unwavering support. You stood beside me through the crash and the climb back. None of this exists without you.

A heartfelt thank you to Kae Wagner, whose partnership, creativity, and editorial brilliance helped transform my raw ideas into a structured narrative that leaders could not only understand but feel. Your instinct for clarity and emotional truth created the container for this book to exist. Working with you was a gift.

And finally, to you, the reader.

Thank you for your willingness to look inward, to examine what's difficult, and to consider the possibility that leadership can be powerful without being punishing. Your presence here means the work has already begun.

May the insights you've gained in these pages support you, steady you, and guide you toward the reset you deserve.

About the Author

Julien Godbarge is a leadership advisor and former C-suite executive who has spent decades inside fast-moving organizations navigating growth, pressure, and the unseen costs of performance. His work centers on decision-making, executive resilience, and the blind spots that quietly shape leaders long before results begin to falter.

Julien brings lived experience and thoughtful perspective to his writing, combining real-world leadership insight with uncommon candor. He works with executives and leadership teams to strengthen clarity, capacity, and sustainable impact, without burnout or bravado.

Glossary

SECTION 1: PSYCHOLOGICAL & EMOTIONAL TERMS

Adaptive Capacity

Your internal ability to handle stress, pressure, and complexity without collapsing into old patterns. High adaptive capacity often comes from emotional regulation, strong identity boundaries, and support systems.

Amygdala Hijack

A fast, automatic emotional reaction triggered when the brain detects threat. This response often bypasses rational thinking and leads to impulsive judgments or defensive behavior.

Atlas Syndrome

The tendency to carry everything alone and avoid asking for help. Leaders with this pattern assume responsibility for more than is sustainable and often feel isolated or burdened.

Basal Ganglia

The part of the brain responsible for habit formation and

automatic behaviors. It explains why insight alone does not change patterns without practice.

Blind Spot

A recurring pattern of behavior or emotion that impacts leadership but operates outside conscious awareness. Blind spots are protective at first but become limiting as responsibilities grow.

Boundary Collapse

When the lines between work and personal life dissolve, leading to emotional fatigue, identity erosion, and chronic overextension.

Cognitive Overload

A mental state where the brain is processing too much information, reducing clarity, slowing decision-making, and increasing emotional reactivity.

Consensus Illusion

When a group appears aligned because everyone agrees outwardly, while true clarity and focus are missing. Often confused with real strategic alignment.

Confirmation Bias

The tendency to interpret information in ways that confirm existing beliefs or emotional states, often deepening blind spots.

Emotional Regulation

The capacity to notice, understand, and manage your emotions in real time without suppressing them or being overwhelmed by them.

Embodiment

Turning insight into consistent behavior. Embodiment occurs when new emotional patterns become the default, not the effort.

Endogenous Pressure

Pressure that comes from within, identity, expectation, fear, rather than external deadlines or demands.

Groupthink

A psychological phenomenon where the desire for harmony overrides the need for critical thinking, leading to poor decisions or lack of true focus.

Hedonic Adaptation

The brain's tendency to quickly normalize successes and return to a baseline, causing leaders to chase achievement without sustained satisfaction.

Identity Fusion

When your sense of self becomes overly tied to your role, performance, or productivity. This often leads to burnout and emotional fragility.

Internal Story

The narrative your mind creates to explain experiences, often unconsciously. These stories reinforce blind spots and shape emotional reactions.

Nervous System Activation

Physiological responses (heart rate, tension, restlessness) triggered by pressure or threat. Chronic activation leads to burnout.

Perfectionism

A fear-based strategy that seeks safety through flawlessness. It often appears productive but leads to exhaustion and stalled execution.

Prefrontal Cortex

The part of the brain responsible for clarity, decision-making, and emotional regulation. It goes offline during high stress or emotional overload.

Psychological Safety

A team environment where people feel safe to speak honestly, admit uncertainty, and challenge ideas without fear of judgment or punishment.

Reactive Leadership

Leadership driven by emotion, urgency, or threat rather than grounded intention, clarity, or strategic perspective.

Regulation

The process of calming and stabilizing the emotional and physiological system so that clarity and choice become possible again.

Self-Correction Trap

The belief that increased effort, intelligence, or willpower alone can break long-standing patterns. Blind spots require support, not force.

Underlying Dynamics

The internal forces, emotional, neurological, and psychological, that sustain a blind spot beneath conscious awareness.

SECTION 2: BUSINESS & LEADERSHIP TERMS

Terms referenced in the Jason Marchand storyline

5S Boards

A lean manufacturing visual management system that organizes workspaces through five principles: Sort, Set in order, Shine, Standardize, and Sustain. Used to improve efficiency and reduce waste.

Alignment

When a team agrees on direction, priorities, or goals. True alignment includes clarity, ownership, and shared understanding, not just verbal agreement in meetings.

Bandwidth

The emotional, mental, or operational capacity available for additional work or responsibility. Leaders often misjudge their own bandwidth, especially during burnout cycles.

Board Packet

A comprehensive document prepared for board members

before formal board meetings. It includes updates on performance, strategy, financials, risks, and key decisions.

C-Suite

The top executive team in an organization that starts with the term: Chief. Typically Chief Executive Officer, Chief Operating Officer, Chief Financial Officer, Chief Technology Officer, Chief Marketing Officer, and others. These roles carry the highest strategic and operational responsibility.

Cadence

The rhythm or frequency of meetings, updates, or strategic reviews. Establishing cadence helps teams maintain momentum and accountability.

Change Management

The structured process of guiding individuals and organizations through transitions in strategy, structure, technology, or culture.

Conflict Avoidance

A leadership pattern where discomfort is minimized at the cost of clarity, honesty, or long-term strategic health. Often mistaken for collaboration.

Corporate Governance

The systems, structures, and policies that guide how decisions are made within an organization and how accountability flows.

CRM (Customer Relationship Management)

A software system that tracks interactions with customers and prospects, managing sales pipelines, contact information, and business relationships. Essential for scaling sales operations.

Cross-Functional Team

A team composed of members from different departments (e.g., product, engineering, marketing) brought together to solve complex problems.

Decision Fatigue

The cognitive exhaustion that results from making too many decisions, often leading to slower thinking, weaker judgment, and reactive leadership.

EBITDA (Earnings Before Interest, Taxes, Depreciation, and Amortization)

A financial metric measuring a company's operating profitability before accounting for financing costs, tax obligations, and non-cash expenses. The holy grail number in private equity deals.

ERP (Enterprise Resource Planning)

Integrated software that manages core business processes including accounting, inventory, purchasing, and operations. The backbone system for running a scaled business.

Executive Sponsor

A senior leader who provides support, visibility, resources, and political backing to a project or initiative.

Focus Drift

The gradual erosion of strategy due to unclear priorities, too many goals, or competing agendas. Appears slowly but impacts execution significantly.

Inventory Turns

A financial ratio measuring how many times inventory is sold and replaced during a period. Higher turns typically indicate efficient operations and strong sales.

Key Performance Indicators (KPIs)

Quantifiable measures used to evaluate the success of a project, role, or organization. KPIs vary depending on goals and industry.

Leadership Debt

The accumulation of delayed decisions, unresolved conflicts, and unaddressed team dynamics that eventually slow execution and increase organizational strain.

Lehman Scale

A standard fee structure for finder's fees or transaction commissions, typically calculated as a percentage of deal value: 5% on the first million, 4% on the second, 3% on the third, 2% on the fourth, and 1% thereafter. Named after Lehman Brothers.

LOI (Letter of Intent)

A preliminary agreement outlining the key terms of a proposed business transaction before final due diligence and legal documentation. Once signed, it signals serious commitment to a deal.

Managing Up

The practice of proactively communicating, influencing, and supporting leaders above you to create alignment and maintain clarity.

Margin Expansion

The strategic effort to increase profitability by raising prices, reducing costs, or improving operational efficiency. A primary focus in private equity value creation.

OKR System (Objectives and Key Results)

A goal-setting framework that establishes clear objectives and measurable key results, fostering transparency and alignment across an organization.

Operational Silos

Departments or teams that work in isolation, limiting collaboration and preventing unified decision-making.

Organizational Drift

A subtle but persistent loss of direction caused by unclear strategy, shifting priorities, or lack of sustained focus.

Performance Review Cycle

The annual or quarterly structured process in which employees are evaluated, given feedback, and aligned on goals and development plans.

Pipeline

In business contexts, can refer to the sales pipeline, product pipeline, or talent pipeline, essentially a flow of future opportunities or resources.

Prioritization Framework

A structured method for determining what work matters most. Often misused or ignored, leading to focus fallacy.

Private Equity Firm

An investment company that pools capital from institutional investors to acquire controlling stakes in businesses, improve operations, and eventually sell for a profit. Masters of the roll-up strategy.

Red Flag

A warning or sign that something is off, culturally, operationally, or emotionally, often noticed but not addressed until it escalates.

Roll-Up

A growth strategy where a company acquires multiple smaller competitors in the same industry, consolidating market share and achieving economies of scale. The faster you roll, the bigger the exit.

RSUs (Restricted Stock Units)

Company shares granted to employees that vest over time, aligning personal wealth with company performance. The carrot that keeps executives focused on exit multiples.

Run Rate

A financial projection extrapolating current performance over a longer period (e.g., estimating annual revenue based on quarterly results).

Strategic Focus

A disciplined commitment to a limited number of priorities that create the greatest impact. Requires saying no far more often than yes.

Succession Planning

Preparing for future leadership transitions by identifying and developing internal candidates or external prospects.

Swim Lanes

Clear ownership boundaries in roles and responsibilities that prevent overlap, confusion, and misalignment in execution.

Traction

Early signs that a project, product, or strategy is working, often measured through customer growth, adoption, revenue, or engagement metrics.

Turnover Risk

The likelihood that a key employee or leader will leave, often heightened when trust erodes or burnout escalates.

Workload Compression

A sudden increase in responsibilities or deadlines without a proportional increase in time or support, often leading to burnout.

www.ingramcontent.com/pod-product-compliance
Lightning Source LLC
LaVergne TN
LVHW100525110826
845146LV00002B/778